1960 1961 1962 1963

1968 1969 1970 1971

1976 1977 1978 1979

1984 1985 1986 1987

1992 1993 1994 1995

2000 2001 2002 2003

2008 2009 2010 2011

2016 2017 2018

DELIUS KLASING

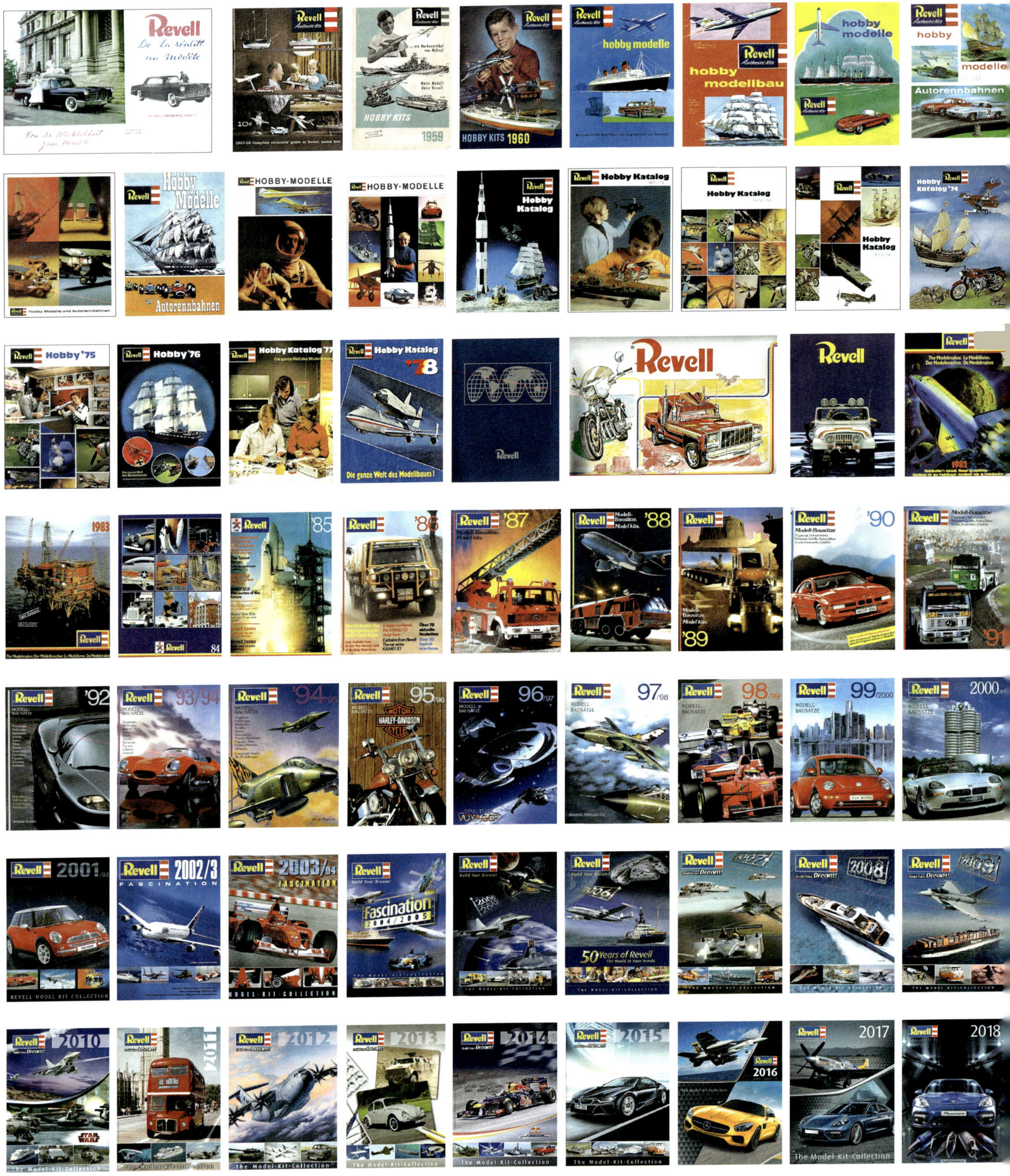

Revell
De la réalité au modèle
Revell Authentic Kits
HOBBY KITS
1959
HOBBY KITS 1960
hobby modelle
hobby modellbau
hobby modelle
modelle
Autorennbahnen
Hobby Modelle
Autorennbahnen
HOBBY-MODELLE
HOBBY-MODELLE
Hobby Katalog
Hobby Katalog
Hobby Katalog
Hobby Katalog
Hobby Katalog '74
Hobby '75
Hobby '76
Hobby Katalog '77
Hobby Katalog '78
Die ganze Welt des Modellbaues!
Revell
Revell
Revell
1983
84
'85
'86
'87
'88
'89
'90
'91
'92
93/94
'94/95
HARLEY-DAVIDSON MOTOR CYCLES
95/96
96/97
VOYAGER
97/98
98/99
99/2000
2000/01
2001/02
2002/3
FASCINATION
2003/04
FASCINATION
Fascination 2004/2005
50 Years of Revell
2007
2008
2009
2010
2011
2012
2013
2014
2015
2016
2017
The Model Kit Collection
2018

ULLI TAUBERT / ANDREAS A. BERSE

The Revell Story

A MODEL OF SUCCESS

DELIUS KLASING VERLAG

Contents

Strong start: From the outset, the Revell model-making label proves to be very creative. One of the first products is a miniaturized atomic power plant (above) and also the first VW bus in a scale of 1:25 (below).

Broad range: Over the course of its history, Revell's range expands steadily, not least thanks to the Bünde branch: accessories such as the Airbrush (left), Star Wars kits (above), 1:18 pre-assembled models such as the BMW Isetta (bottom left) or pirate ships that glow mysteriously in the dark (below).

Creativity counts

For more than 60 years, Revell has been a success story of creativity – with our customers and within our own company.

Man's desire to create something lasting is as old as humanity itself. Even the oldest known artifacts from human culture are testimony to the creativity of our species. Throughout the ages, techniques, materials and, above all, objects that were always relicts of their time have changed.

When Revell first "saw the light of day" mid last century, it didn't take long before creative people discovered that Revell was the brand that helped them live their dreams and allowed them to enjoy their hobby. However, modelmaking wasn't the only hobby in which Revell was involved. This book outlines the anecdotes and adventures of the last 70 years since the founding of the company in Venice, California. It's a gripping story not only of a company that has become the epitome of plastic kits, but also one that "migrated" to other continents and kept reinventing itself with new products.

Building the future: Stefan Krings took over the helm of the kit flagship Revell in January 2016 and is determined to steer the market leader in creativity into the future with new product lines.

This book allows a glimpse into the world of those dedicated people who stand behind the Revell name. And I, who had the great fortune of meeting some of these people personally, can underline that this Revell brand is the product of great and devoted people. They have all followed the values of the brand, exactly as I'd always imagined when I joined the company in January 2016.

The stories in this book are fascinating, true and moving. They prove why the brand and the company have inspired employees and model builders for decades, and will continue to do so. I wish you a great deal of enjoyment as you dip into the enthralling history of Revell and perhaps we'll meet personally some day at a trade fair, at your favorite model kit shop, or at the place where you indulge your Revell creativity.

Warm regards, Stefan Krings

Getting the hang of it: Junior Kits are one of the new product lines of Revell Germany that clearly points a way to the future. Shown here is the Lightning McQueen car from the successful and internationally renowned Disney movie Cars, which can also be easily assembled by very young modelmakers.

Jaap has lots of boxes

Model kit collector Jaap Zwart from the Netherlands is not just a nice guy. Without him, it would have been all but impossible to make this Revell book.

While researching for this book I was also on the lookout for vintage kits that we had not yet archived at Revell. The background: Revell's archive only started in the mid-seventies with the completion of our new building – before this there was simply no suitable space. Hence, Revell only began archiving in earnest from this point in time.

Over the years I've hunted high and low for collectors for this book who were willing to help us find those missing models from the early years. An old friend, Gert Vlaanderen from IPMS Netherlands, offered to help me and put a request for collectors to contact him in his magazine Modelbouw in Plastic. We were lucky. Jaap Zwart agreed to give us his full support. We arranged an appointment at very short notice, sent a wish list of old model kits we were trying to track down, which we then wanted to photograph at his home. What the author found at Jaap's house simply took his breath away.

The Revell collector: Jaap Zwart, shown here on the left with Revell veteran Ulli Taubert, has collected over 2,500 of the brand's vintage model kits over the years.

By irony of fate, it took me 50 years of working at Revell to meet the man who officially owns the world's largest and most complete collection of our products from 1942 to 1967. The truly most valuable models are the first toys from the pre-1945 era: products and model kits that even I had never seen before. In his collection, Jaap had merchandise from a time when Revell kits had not yet arrived in the USA, just toys to buy. And from 1949, at the start of model kit production, he acquired everything that came on the market there. Insiders know that there is a whole series of products, pre-1956 and beyond, that never found their way onto the German market, model kits like the much sought-after aircraft and ship sets. Also in Jaap Zwart's incredible collection are extremely rare and now priceless gems such as the Atomic Power Plant and the Space Station.

Even before Revell itself became active on the Dutch market with its own travelling salesmen, Jaap had

Magnificent assortment: Jaap Zwart has been an acknowledged Revell chronologist for decades. Although he enjoys assembling the plastic kits (see above) – and this is the key to his collection – he usually leaves the vintage model sets unopened and keeps them well-preserved on shelves.

---

obtained all the Revell kits through the respective importers, first Suls, then Tenco. Jaap, too, has his own interesting story. The sprightly Dutchman, now in his late seventies, was born in 1940 in Surabaya, those days part of the Dutch East Indies. His father was a member of the Dutch Navy and was captured by the Japanese during the occupation. He and his mother were also detained. After the war he arrived in Singapore, where he lived near the Changi Royal Air Force airfield, and developed an interest in the aircraft and flying boats that were stationed there.

And that was when he was bitten by the aircraft bug. After several years, his parents moved back to the Netherlands very close to an airport near Hilversum. As a child he used to cycle to nearby airports with his camera and take photos. Jaap has stayed true to his hobby all his life. On the side, he also compiled a formidable collection of model kit sets – with a preference for Revell products – now totaling around 2,500 models. Note: Write a book and you get to meet the nicest people.

Ulli Taubert

Yeah! Yeah! Yeah!

Yes, it's true: Revell also made the legendary Beatles in a scale of 1:8 and not out of 'Norwegian Wood'!

Shortly after I started working at Revell in 1968 I noticed something peculiar that many modelers are unaware of even today: one catalog, namely from 1965, features an illustration of the Beatles, four individual figurines on a scale of 1:8 – as plastic model kits. I managed to buy the one remaining kit privately. However, during my many years at Revell, this matter continued to play on my mind. Over the course of my career I obtained a second kit from the bankruptcy assets of a German toy retailer, and subsequently had the other two figures sent from abroad.

Today, I can call all "Fab Four" my own, each still unassembled in their original packaging. In the seventies, I tried to locate where the tools were made and I found out that they had traveled from Venice/California in 1986 with the entire Revell molds to the Monogram facility in Chicago and they were still there. We then brought two tools back to Bünde – each mold included two figures – and we tested them. The quality was excellent and Revell then did all it could to reissue them.

John Lennon's widow was always the one to hamper this initiative. We only had permission to portray the Beatles as a comic adaption of the movie Yellow Submarine, but we didn't want that. While writing this book, I became interested in the background story of the Beatles. I had to refer to existing literature, especially the works of Thomas Graham and Jean-Christophe Carbonel, who both made mention of this topic in their respective Revell books.

In 1963, the year the Beatles made their breakthrough in England, Lewis "Lew" and Royle Glaser visited the Potters Bar branch as part of their European tour. During their stay in England, they discovered that people, particularly teenage girls, screamed hysterically at the wild concerts of a band called The Beatles. The Glasers liked neither the group's moptop hairstyle nor their music, but were convinced that it wouldn't be long before the Beatles phenomenon made its way across the pond to America.

Back in New York, the pair popped in to the newly opened Beatles office and signed an exclusive contract for hobby products for the U.S. market. Royle was convinced that she'd finally found a product for the company's female target group. The contract came with a 15 percent cut instead of Revell's customary five percent. Because of this license fee, the contract was initially capped at just one year, which is why the figurines can only be found in the catalog and price list of 1965. In 1966 they disappeared from

Revellution: In 1965, the 'Fab Four' made their debut in the Revell catalog – in spite of the record license fee for those times. Revell thought they'd found an ideal product for girls with the figurines – which very quickly proved to be a mistake.

---

the catalog, with only three figures (excluding Ringo) mentioned in the price list. Royle Glaser gave herself a pat on the back for this coup, but later admitted: "I was surprised that the figurines weren't popular."

Thus, it came about that these characters were sold predominantly in the USA and only in small quantities. Only a few boxes made it to Europe. Today, the four figures are sought-after treasures that fetch phenomenal prices amongst collectors and at auctions. Far out!

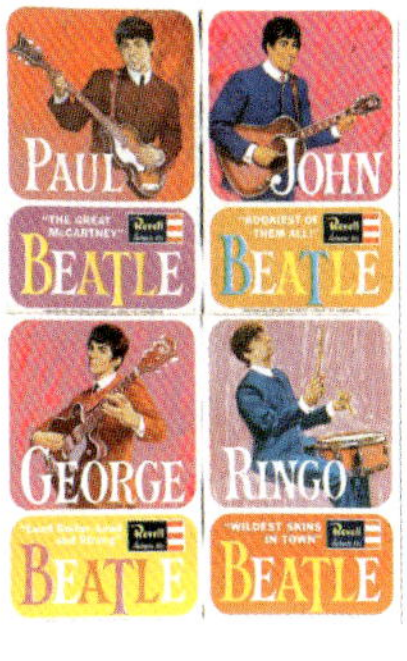

Whether it's John, Paul, George or Ringo: Today, the 1:8-scale Beatles model kits from Revell are extremely rare collectors' items.

Dazzling: With its Beatles packaging, Revell succeeded in creating a small pop art masterpiece. Well-preserved boxes boost the already high value enormously.

The plastics pioneer

The story of Revell Deutschland began on a wet and cold March day in Nuremberg and Heinz-Georg Schöneberg was in the right place at the right time.

The door of the Hotel Deutscher Kaiser in Nuremberg swung open and a cold, damp wind swept through the room. A small man in a coat, his collar turned up and his hat pulled low over his forehead, entered the lobby as if stepping from the movie *The Third Man*. It was Lewis "Lew" H. Glaser and under his arm he carried a parcel, whose contents would transform children's bedrooms for the next three generations: plastic kits – made in the USA.

Great teamwork: After founding Revell Plastics in 1956, the managing director Heinz-Georg Schöneberg immediately puts together a strong team of employees.

In the pleasantly warm hotel lounge, Heinz-Georg Schöneberg sat with three colleagues from the company Richard Schreiber, a successful toy retailer of that time. Schöneberg, as it would turn out, had definitely picked the right time and the right place – and his English wasn't half bad either. He greeted the new arrival warmly, helped him check-in to his room, and asked the American what he had in his package.

The mystery was quickly revealed. Glaser was given the chance to showcase his plastic model kits 'unofficially' to the German public at the Schreiber stand at a toy fair, where Schöneberg and his colleagues would then sell them. When the German sold almost three times more in the north than his colleagues did in the south over the next months, one thing became clear: If Lewis Glaser ever decided to establish a German subsidiary of his Revell company, Schöneberg would be the managing director. Thus, not long after, Glaser decided to set up a distribution warehouse in Germany. The time was ripe in 1956: The German company Revell Plastics was listed in the trade register in Bielefeld, and the company began operations in an old cigar factory on the Kaiser-Wilhelm-Straße in the town of Bünde. This year, Schöneberg would have turned 86 years old. As the undisputed pioneer at Revell Deutschland, he built from scratch a business that would eventually achieve international fame. It took, however, quite some time before he traveled to his first meeting in the land of endless opportunity:

Germany's chief: At Schreiber, Heinz-Georg Schöneberg sells more Revell goods than any other salesman. As managing director, the self-made man determinedly continues to strengthen the position of Revell Germany.

Schöneberg, a former Heinkel bomber pilot, traveled by boat, his youngest daughter Andrea recalls. There was no way he would entrust his life to some pilot he didn't know. He and Lewis Glaser clicked immediately and over the years they established a deep, lasting friendship.

The mood in Germany at this time was optimistic and the Revell products sold like hotcakes. When the staffing situation in the distribution department became tight, the sales staff would throw on some overalls after hours and help out with the packaging. This was the time of the so-called economic miracle. Standing at the forefront of all this was "Uncle" Schöneberg, as the workers fondly called behind closed doors. He was also a visionary. Very soon, when the cigar factory premises became too cramped, Revell moved out. Thanks once again to Schöneberg, the company found its permanent headquarters in the early seventies in the industrial area on Henschelstraße.

In the truest sense of the word, Schöneberg was a patriarch and had earned a great deal of respect. Ulli Taubert, development guru amongst the East-Westphalians, recalls: "When I received my first invitation to the company party, I made very sure that my suit and tie were looking perfect." However, the manager also knew how to celebrate. On one occasion, Marlène Charell danced as the main attraction at a Revell reception one evening on the occasion of the toy fair at Nuremberg. And, Schöneberg had a knack of bringing the right people together. Kurt Haubrok earned his trust, and many other Revell veterans joined the model kit manufacturer at a young age and stayed in East Westphalia for a long time.

Bosom buddies: Revell founder Lewis "Lew" Glaser (left) and Schöneberg develop a very close bond.

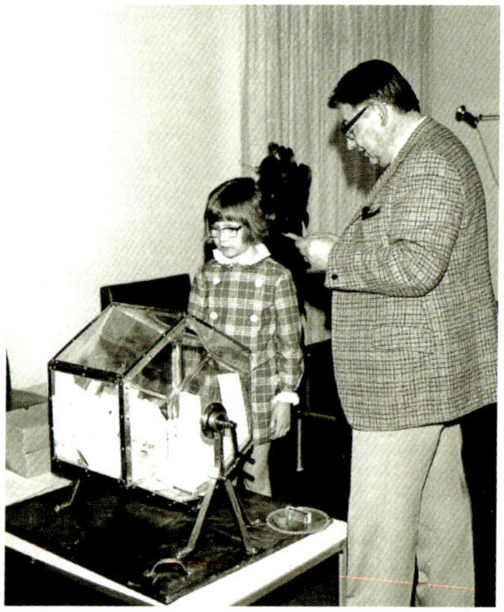

The marketing expert: Heinz-Georg Schöneberg's first goal is to make Revell a household name. Thus, the PR specialist also enjoys organizing raffles.

Uncle Schöneberg also knew how to be thrifty. When the dollar exchange rate made the Revell model kits, which were still shipped from the USA in the sixties, extremely expensive, he and Haubrok came up with a simple yet ingenious idea to save money. Revell Germany only bought the filled plastic bags from the United States, but the construction manuals and packaging were "Made in Germany". This shaved 30 percent off the price and boosted sales. In fact, this marked the start for Revell Germany to make the first cut of the still tightly tied apron strings to the parent company in the USA. Revell established its strong position in the retail sector, where it remained loyal to specialist retailers and avoided, if possible, delivering to big supermarkets and wholesalers into the seventies. Schöneberg also recognized the value of accessories and hence sold the Humbrol range of colors. Eventually Revell would create its own paints. Revell's first foray into the Benelux region also began during his era.

When Lewis Glaser died on September 12, 1972, and his wife took over the business, the relationship with the United States cooled considerably. Heinz-Georg Schöneberg probably realized rather quickly that Royle Glaser was overburdened with the leadership of the US parent company and he was candid in expressing his opinion. The situation exploded in 1978, long before the sale of Revell Germany to Céji, and Schöneberg washed his hands of the whole business. Setting up his own consulting business, he stayed true to the toy industry, advising such well-known brands as Steiff, Ravensburger and Märklin.

Meeting of experts: Schöneberg (right) also relishes intense discussions with Lewis Glaser from America (center) about the future product policies of the fledgling model kit brand, Revell.

Big wigs at the fair: Karl Schiller himself visits the Revell stand at the Nuremberg toy fair. Such ministerial visitors raises the profile of German toy manufacturers.

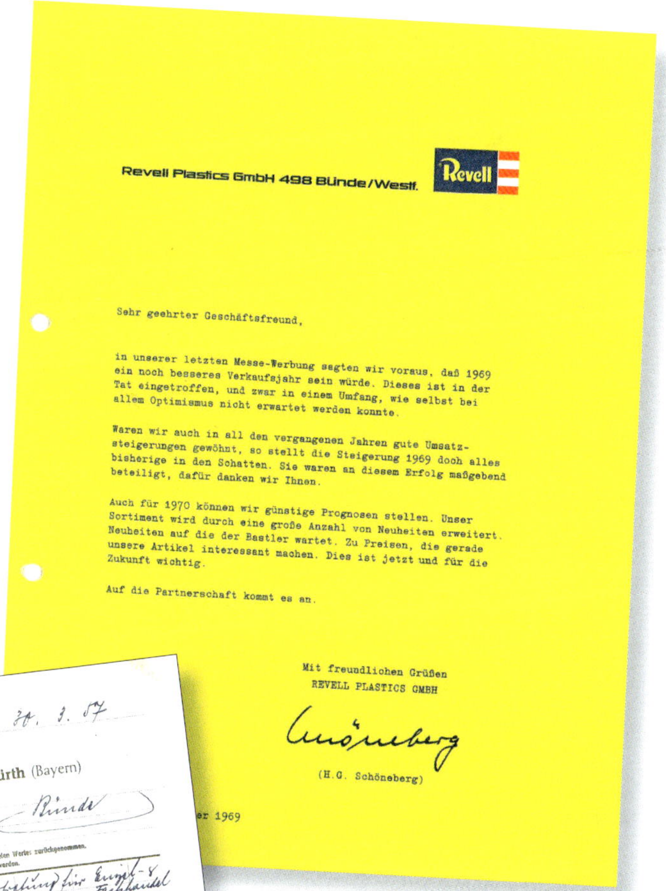

Revell Plastics GmbH 498 Bünde/Westf.

Sehr geehrter Geschäftsfreund,

in unserer letzten Messe-Werbung sagten wir voraus, daß 1969 ein noch besseres Verkaufsjahr sein würde. Dieses ist in der Tat eingetroffen, und zwar in einem Umfang, wie selbst bei allem Optimismus nicht erwartet werden konnte.

Waren wir auch in all den vergangenen Jahren gute Umsatzsteigerungen gewöhnt, so stellt die Steigerung 1969 doch alles bisherige in den Schatten. Sie waren an diesem Erfolg maßgebend beteiligt, dafür danken wir Ihnen.

Auch für 1970 können wir günstige Prognosen stellen. Unser Sortiment wird durch eine große Anzahl von Neuheiten erweitert. Neuheiten auf die der Bastler wartet. Zu Preisen, die gerade unsere Artikel interessant machen. Dies ist jetzt und für die Zukunft wichtig.

Auf die Partnerschaft kommt es an.

Mit freundlichen Grüßen
REVELL PLASTICS GMBH

(H.G. Schöneberg)

...er 1969

Avid traveler: No road is too long for Heinz-Georg Schöneberg when it comes to promoting the products of Revell Germany.

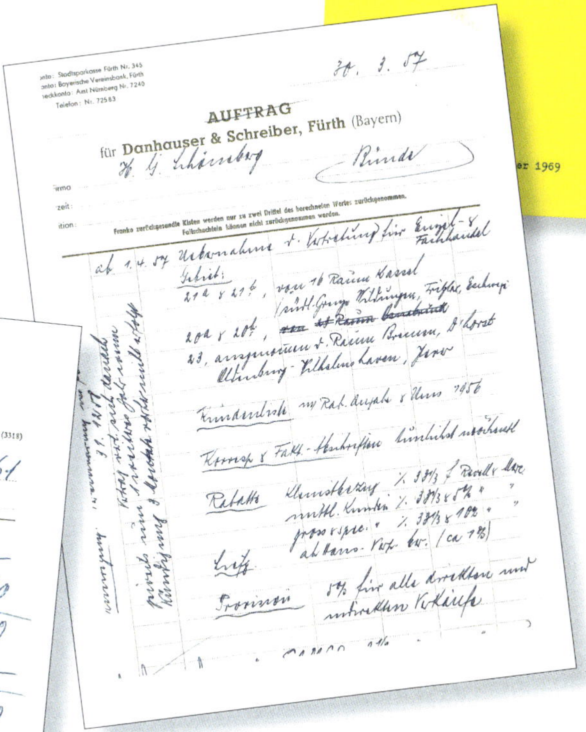

AUFTRAG
für Danhauser & Schreiber, Fürth (Bayern)

H. G. Schöneberg — Bünde

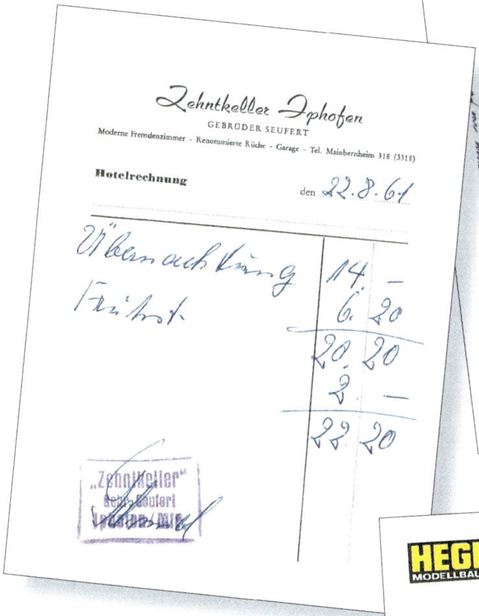

Zehntkeller Iphofen
GEBRÜDER SEUFERT
Moderne Fremdenzimmer · Renommierte Küche · Garage · Tel. Mainbernheim 318 (3318)

Hotelrechnung den 22.8.61

Übernachtung	14.–
Frühst.	6.20
	20.20
	2.–
	22.20

Well-known: In the toy industry, Heinz-Georg Schöneberg earns himself an impeccable reputation as a very fair business partner.

HEGI MODELLBAU

HEINZ-GEORG SCHÖNEBERG
Geschäftsführender Gesellschafter

Kaiser-Wilhelm-Straße 19 · D-4980 Bünde 1 · Tel. (0 52 23) 67 42

Mrs H G Schoneberg

Farewell Party

Revell Authentic Kits

THURSDAY, 15th JULY 1965
JACK STRAW'S CASTLE, HAMPSTEAD HEATH, LONDON N.W.3, ENGLAND

Highly classified kits

In the realization of projects, Revell had to overcome many hurdles. Sometimes even with the Secret Services.

Do sneaky spies work at Revell? As unbelievable as it may sound, Revell occasionally ran into difficulties with American security agencies. Although these problems always had to do with models in some small way, there were at times incredible incidences that the public never heard about, until now. This was also because in every case the American parent was always the target of investigations. I personally only know these stories from hearsay, albeit straight from the mouths of those who were involved at Revell in the USA. It all started relatively early, when Revell launched the first nuclear-powered submarine kit on the U.S. market in 1956, the USS Nautilus (H-308). Revell had a visit from several gentlemen who insisted on hearing how the company got hold of original drawings for the tool design. This was in the Cold War era and the military topic was treated with a great deal of sensitivity. Even then, Revell's developers could prove that everything was above board and the team had taken the official line with all necessary approvals.

Bearer of secrets: With stealth bombers like the F-117, Revell is sometimes faster launching its model kits than the American intelligence agencies are happy with.

The next episode came in 1978 after we published our catalog with the title page showing the new Boeing 747 piggyback model with the Space Shuttle (H-177). Once again, several American "gentlemen" reacted somewhat sensitively, with our U.S. colleagues across the pond asked to disclose the information source for this project. Here, too, everything was on the level and they eventually found out how we knew about the contents of the shuttle's interior. Indeed, what we had implemented was fictional and not real.

However, the biggest problems in this regard happened in 1983 with the new aircraft development that we'd initiated in Bünde. It was the F-19 Stealth Fighter, a concept design of the emerging "stealth" theme. At that time, our company received the famous Jane's Report of International Defence every year from the USA. In it was a small picture of the

Revell's X-files: The U.S. authorities first become aware of the Revell company in 1956, when the Americans release their model kits of the ultra-modern USS Nautilus submarine with very skillfully executed detailing.

Dive, dive, dive: Although the USS Nautilus's interior has no technology, Revell's plastic kit set from 1956 attracts the attention of the secret service. And the kit producer remains on the radar of the relevant authorities in the United States for a long time.

Stealth Fighter (4740), and we'd invented the F-19 designation because this was the successive number to the real design. We then developed a 1:32-scale model based on a small picture, and this upset the men in black. It should also be said that this model never made it to the market. The finished miniature looked nothing like the final aircraft design that went into production.

Secret blueprints: In Germany, the submarine blueprints hit the headlines, and Revell comes under suspicion of the national espionage agency with miniature aircraft.

The next incident came in 1987. Also from Jane's Report we took the concept of an ominous B-2 Stealth Bomber (4577), which everyone was talking about at that time. It was to replace the extremely expensive B-1. Once again, intelligence agents knocked at our door of our unsuspecting colleagues in America. Despite all the problems, the model went into production and became one of the most successful products for many years. This model was also miles away from the eventual reality.

In 1988, we again took the F-19 Stealth Fighter illustrated in the Jane's Report and developed it to the scales 1:48 (4580) and 1:144 (4051) in parallel. Here, again, came the obligatory enquiries from the authorities. Yet, the 1:144 model in particular turned into one of the best-sellers of the entire program, and this continued for a very long time, even when the real Stealth Fighter F-117 joined the program.

This was then added to the collection in 1990 as 1:144 and 1:72 models. Once again, the secret services turned up immediately, although the model was only launched at the end of the production run. They tried to keep all the documents like drawings and information secret during the time of production, but it was all in vain. Several details went public

Much ado about nothing: The Revell product developers take most of their inspiration for their secret projects from the International Defense Review, a regularly published magazine that includes future developments in the aircraft and ship sectors in great detail.

---

and this enabled us to create at least a semi-decent model, but it wasn't perfect.

The last known incident on this subject took place in 1956 when we reconstructed the first US Navy Stealth Ship Sea Shadow (5088) again from photos out of Jane's and other magazines. Although we didn't receive any documentation at that time, we were able to develop the model according to the correct dimensions but it was impossible to get any details of the interior. The real ship was ultimately used for some years as a development mule for the US Navy. The model proved less successful due to its unspectacular design and the fact that no weaponry was used. Around the year 2000, we changed procedures so that we always asked after the originator and subsequently received approval or a license agreement – as well as supplying all design details, of course.

Ulli Taubert

Revell gives the green light!

As a revenue boost, Revell in the USA also focused on the H0-gauge train theme in the mid-fifties – still a little-known chapter in the story of the model kit brand.

It's time to shed some light on a topic that has never before been discussed in Europe, but one that has played a role in the USA. I'm talking about the American idea of breaking into the H0-gauge railway market. The author first came across this on the back cover of the 1957/58 catalog and immediately became curious. Reference was made to Revell H0 Electric Trains. By sending in a dime, each customer could request a separate catalog with these products. Sadly, I never sent my 10 cents. I was all the more surprised when I happened to meet up with my orthopedist, Oliver Jeike, while researching for this book. He is the son of our former dispatch manager. We started to talk, and of course the topic of Revell arose. He told me that when his father died he'd left him several Revell train sets. In disbelief, I asked him if he was mistaken and perhaps meant car racetracks. At that time I'd heard almost nothing of railway sets. We arranged to meet privately. What Oliver Jeike revealed took my breath away: an entire box filled with heirloom rolling stock. They were indeed the Revell H0 Electric Trains, all from 1956. They were all typical American wagons, plus some buildings from 1958 to 1960 model kits. We spent a long time talking about their history. The upshot of this is that Oliver Jeike placed these antiquities at our disposal and they immediately took pride of place in Revell's in-house archives at Bünde.

Well on track: At the end of the fifties, Revell becomes involved in the railway business. For the H0 Electric Trains, customers could order a catalog for a dime. Some of the buildings ultimately find their way to Germany.

My research then revealed that Revell Inc. in the United States had been looking for a partner to collaborate with for this H0 project and found Rivarossi in Italy. This turned out to be the reason why the range was never available in Europe. The buildings, however, were built and developed by the American company Concor. These were sold under the Revell Authentic Scale Buildings logo.

The capital expenditure for Revell was said to have come to five million US dollars. However, due to the weak sales of this series, the railroad adventure remained a bad investment. But the story has an epilogue: Early in the collaboration of Revell in Bünde with the company Heljan in Denmark, I noticed

Connecting the world: Although the focus of Revell's railway activities lies in rolling materials made in conjunction with Rivarossi, they also produce buildings specifically for the H0-gauge railway tracks in cooperation with Concor.

Times of change: The box below is from the Revell reissue in Bünde. The bottom image shows the very rare so-called "rolling material".

immediately the many American-looking houses in their kits – and in fact they were from the former US Revell-H0 model kit that Heljan in Denmark had purchased from Revell Inc. in the US and subsequently offered to its customers. The irony of all this was that among these kits were a number of designs that we then bought from Heljan and sold in the mid-eighties as part of Revell Germany's H0 assortment. That's how small the railway world is.

Ulli Taubert

Staging a comeback: The Danish company Heljan later buys many of the building kit sets from the Americans. As fate would have it, the kits would eventually end up in the model kit range of Revell in the East Westphalian town of Bünde.

Chronicle
1956–2018

Building instructions to success

There are several books that tell the story of Revell in the USA. This book, however, is dedicated to the history of Revell Germany, which was first entered in the commercial register at Bielefeld in 1956 before opening for business in the German town of Bünde. The chronology was written by Ulli Taubert, the development specialist at Revell, with the help of Andreas A. Berse and many contemporary witnesses interviewed by a team of authors for this book.

1956

Ships like this harbor tug were part of the Revell model kit range from the very beginning.

After the entry of Revell Plastics GmbH in the Bielefeld commercial register and from August 1956 in the trade register at the Bünde district court, the first Revell catalog appeared on the market. The first small run was initially published in French and German. The reason for the French publication was because a Swiss investor held the majority of the limited liability company shares. This made Switzerland the first country in Europe after Germany to which Revell products were imported from the USA. The still-modest catalog in A5 landscape format measuring 21x15 centimeters with just 20 pages was printed in black and white, with the texts in red. The four-color process was only used for the title and back cover. Instead of a logo, the Revell name was used and this would remain unchanged for many years. The contents of the catalog were also rather modest, but it included model kits that would remain part of the range for decades and today count among the best-selling kit sets worldwide. Examples of these are: Sikorsky S-55 (6.50 DM), U-Boat Nautilus (6.50 DM), Torpedo Boat (7.25 DM), USS Missouri (14.50 DM), Robert E. Lee (14.50 DM), Harbor Tug Long Beach (9.40 DM), Constitution and Bounty (21.80 DM) from the small sailing ship series. The prices of the products were the shop retail prices in German Marks (DM), the currency of that time. Under the slogan "From Reality to Model" and "When a model – then a Revell", the catalog also included some of the very first Revell models from the original Highway Pioneers, plus typical American cars and trucks. Highly popular amongst today's collectors are the old series with a variety of horse-drawn carriages. Inconceivable today, but topical at that time: a small run of true-to-scale historical handguns. And in the back of the catalog were some kits that are highly sought-after today: gift sets, which were simply three different kits.

This first Revell catalog may have been small and rather humble, but it marked the start. Offering kit sets based solely on those of the parent company in the United States, the newcomer in the German model kit market put its visiting card on the table and flew the flag.

In its Navy Log, Revell shows very clearly that it was based on original documents from the US Navy.

1957 & 58

Figures such as Perri the pine squirrel give the Revell range a distinctive character.

With the 1957/58 catalog, the German subsidiary also used the Revell logo for the first time. Over the course of Revell's history, this symbol would receive countless design tweaks, making some unhappy followers suggest it was a violation. More can be read on this topic in a separate story on page 146. The sub-line or slogan "Revell Authentic Kits" would keep its meaning for much longer. The catalog, now published in an eye-catching four-color process, was printed by Revell in America and was also sent to Germany. The 1957/58 edition was only available in English. Since the catalog was also of very high quality compared to the competition of that time, and to keep costs down, Revell printed only one run covering both years. The catalog contained an impressive list of model kits, and the range of the plastic model kit brand continued to boom. Many long-term products were already on offer, two ship model sets were added to the models from 1956: the USS Forrestal and the Santa Maria. All of these products were meticulously categorized to specific themes, not just general Aircraft, but more specifically Air Force Fighters, Navy Fighters, Air Force Bombers, Navy Bombers, Military Transport, Airliners and many more. The fact that they were all packaged in a modern and very appealing design was a persuasive calling card for the fledgling company. New to Revell's products was a military vehicle as well as the return of the entire Highway Pioneers range from the first year of Revell in the USA. These so-called "reissues" were not uncommon in the early days at Revell. Cleverly positioned, they were intended to represent a leitmotiv through the company's program development. The first licensed article also appeared in 1957: Perri the Squirrel from Walt Disney. Another new product, albeit only available in the USA, was a small run of H0-gauge trains – a production line created in collaboration with Rivarossi from Italy. For a dime, you could buy a catalog dedicated solely to Revell H0 Electric Trains.

With an entire armada of stagecoach kits, Revell honors the days of the legendary Wild West.

1959

Already in the early days, Revell ventures into unusual themes like this detailed drawing of a nuclear power station as a model kit.

From 1959, the Revell catalog found a home in Germany. The edition from 1959 was the promotional banner, which was printed by the company Bohlmeier close to Bünde and was also published in German at long last. All images were contemporary illustrations from the Stakelbeck studio in Bünde, which were kept in black and white. This would definitely have cut costs at that time. Still, the 1959 catalog marked a milestone. The world-renowned brand name Revell Authentic Kits was translated into the language of poets and thinkers: *Wenn Modell, dann Revell* (when a model, then a Revell). All novelties of this year were shown on no less than eight pages in the middle of the catalog, making it possible to present these pages as an extra novelty brochure. Due to the political situation, the demand for rockets and missile weapons went sky high – and the same was true at Revell. The first

Revell scales down the HMS Victory sailing ship several times over the years. The first kit comes out in the fifties.

The 1:25-scale kit of the VW Kombi as Micro Bus is one of Revell's first flagship projects and sets the benchmark in terms of detailing.

Right from the outset, Revell has no hesitation in tackling science fiction themes, as this Moon Ship model underlines.

models were launched based on the First World War, including 1:28-scale aircraft. Some of the novelties of that time are now almost priceless collector's items such as the Atomic Power Plant (45.50 DM), two science fiction Space Station kits (32.50 DM), the Moon Ship (6.50 DM) and the legendary Volkswagen bus (9.75 DM). Hot sellers such as the large Cutty Sark (65.00 DM) and the small HMS Victory (19.50 DM) came on the market, as well as the X-15 (5.90 DM) and the large Sopwith Camel (12.95 DM). Still a best-seller today is the USS George Washington with its detailed interior (12.95 DM). I've also listed these products with the price in German Marks. Taking into account that a loaf of bread in 1959 cost about 85 pfennig, it's clear that Revell products of that time were top-of-the-range luxury items compared to today's prices. And it was no wonder at an exchange rate of 4 DM for US$1. Still in the 1959 program but already on their way out were the stagecoaches and pistols. In contrast, the outer space theme was gaining traction. And, typical of Revell, this would continue for six decades: Quickly identifying current developments and turning them into plastic model sets. Technological, political or social developments have also been reflected in model making – a secret of Revell's success.

The tea clipper Cutty Sark follows in the wake of the HMS Victory. Over the course of Revell's history, it too was downsized several times.

With the Sopwith Camel, the Americans tackle another subject that would run like a thread through the model kit range: biplanes.

1960 & 61

Even Peter Pan inspires the product managers at Revell. Thus, the kit of the legendary Jolly Roger pirate ship is created in the early sixties.

This entire catalog was also put together in the town of Bünde. While the inside pages remained black and white, this time the advertisers splashed out with a title in expensive four-color print. The new products of this year were again positioned in the center to enable the separate printing of a news brochure. With this catalog came a new range, the Whip Flying Series. This, however, would have a relatively short lifespan. Youngsters could assemble and launch these special models into the air using a control line. Popular sellers also hit the market, such as the ships Iowa, the Fletcher, the Thermopylae, the Peter Pan, which was available for decades, and the Sea Eagle. The first European cars also appeared, for instance the Porsche Carrera and Mercedes 190 SL in a 1:25 scale as well as an H-900 series with Karmann, Rover and Jaguar in a scale of approximately 1:40, and the Highway Pioneers were continued. The first engine, an Allison Turbo Prop, was also introduced as a 1:10 kit during the year. A little digression at this point: Why do Americans take the 1:25 scale and the Europeans opt for 1:24? The measurement 1:25, half an inch (1.26 centimeters) on the model, corresponds to one foot (30.48 centimeters) in the original. Because the British used a

Dream ships like the Orient ocean liner SS Oriana with its finely detailed plastic kit becomes a regular feature early on in the catalog of the plastic model specialists.

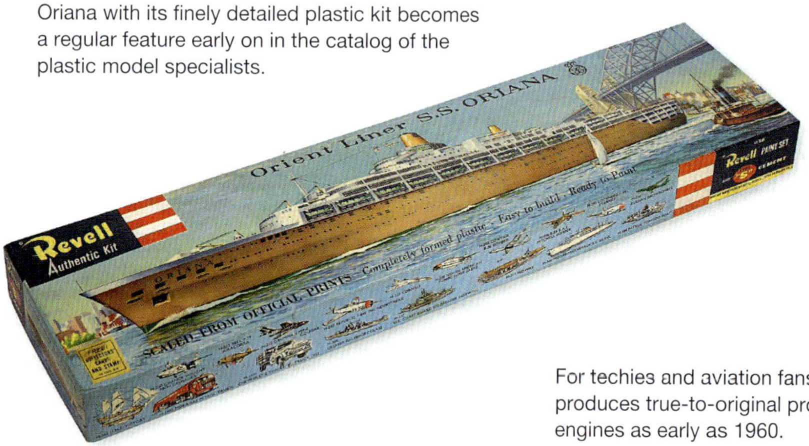

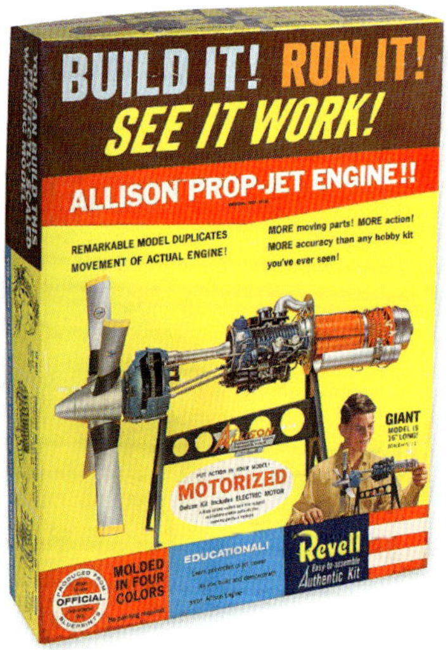

For techies and aviation fans, Revell produces true-to-original prop-jet engines as early as 1960.

Convair F-106A Delta Dart, F-84F and the Russian Pendant Yak-25 plastic model kits from Revell are also suitable as slingshot planes.

London foot instead of the American measurement, Europe settled on 1:24 as the standard. To this day, models from the USA are sometimes delivered as 1:25-scale kits, while those from Europe and Asia come in 1:24.

In 1961, the Revell makers reprinted the catalog from the previous year, but added the year "1961" on the title. At the same time, they added a leaflet showing three new aircraft models, as well as a separate reference to the Whip Flying Series, also known as slingshot planes. For the first time, aircraft offered in a so-called poly bag, particularly inexpensive at 2.95 DM, were intended as competition to the then emerging and popular Airfix kits from England. With the high US dollar, the selling prices of Revell kits were correspondingly high.

To reduce costs, Revell strategists offer kits in a somewhat simpler poly bag packaging.

1962

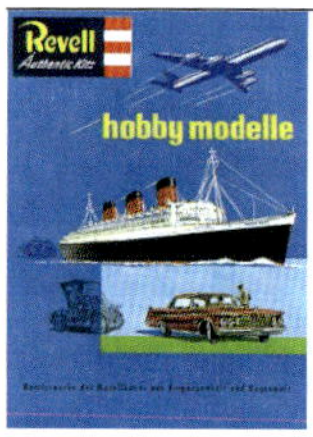

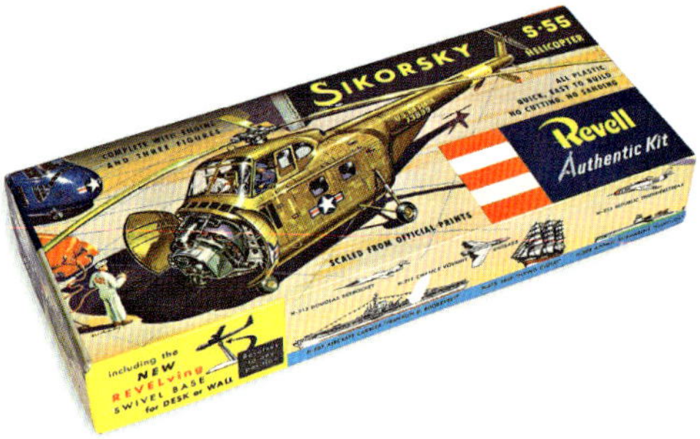

The Sikorsky S-55 marks the start of the helicopter kit era for Revell – including a complete set of figures and an intricate engine.

This catalog, too, was printed in Bünde, with a four-color title again featuring contemporary illustrations courtesy of the Stakelbeck studio. Featured in this catalog were the two first kits tailored specifically by the American parent company for the German market: the H-125 F-84 F Thunderstreak 1:55 and the H-214 Sikorsky S-55 1:40, both in the design of the German Luftwaffe. Country-specific variations from the USA underscored that Germany had now become a significant sales market. This was a compliment for the sales success of Revell Germany in Bünde. Scales at this time did not play a significant role; the products were simply designed to fit in the box, hence scales were unimportant. Today, the plastic model builders like to call such miniatures "rule of thumb" boxes. Other sales hits came on the market like the Queen Mary, the Olympia fire-fighting boat, the Saratoga and the Polaris submarine in 1:253. An additional large engine kit was introduced: a Chrysler 8-cylinder V-shaped motor. And for the Revell parent company in the United States, the subject of accessories played an increasingly important role. Revell were keen to provide hobbyists with more of the tools and materials they needed directly from the factory. Therefore, in 1962, Revell started a long-standing cooperation with the paint manufacturer Humbrol from England. The company based in Hull started out as an oil company and as early as the fifties specialized in the production of paints and other accessories used in the field of model making. These colors then came to Germany in the form of the famous 14-milliliter pots that modelers have surely encountered at some stage in their lives. In contrast to the American parent company, Revell in Germany had already started to develop its own colors by the mid-eighties. What made these accessories particularly attractive was the fact that when the pots were empty, model builders had to buy new ones. As such, accessories became a growing aftermarket commodity.

The "world's most powerful fire-fighter boat" is definitely an appropriate template for the enterprising development team at Revell in the United States.

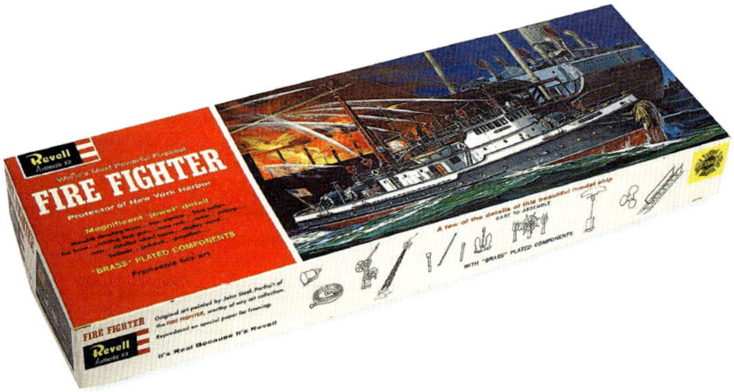

Following the example of Chrysler's six-cylinder inline engine, in 1962, Revell produces a very large 1:4-scale model kit, which is gigantic for that time.

In the opinion of Revell strategists, the Polaris submarine from the so-called Washington Class offers hobbyists a very interesting kit-set model.

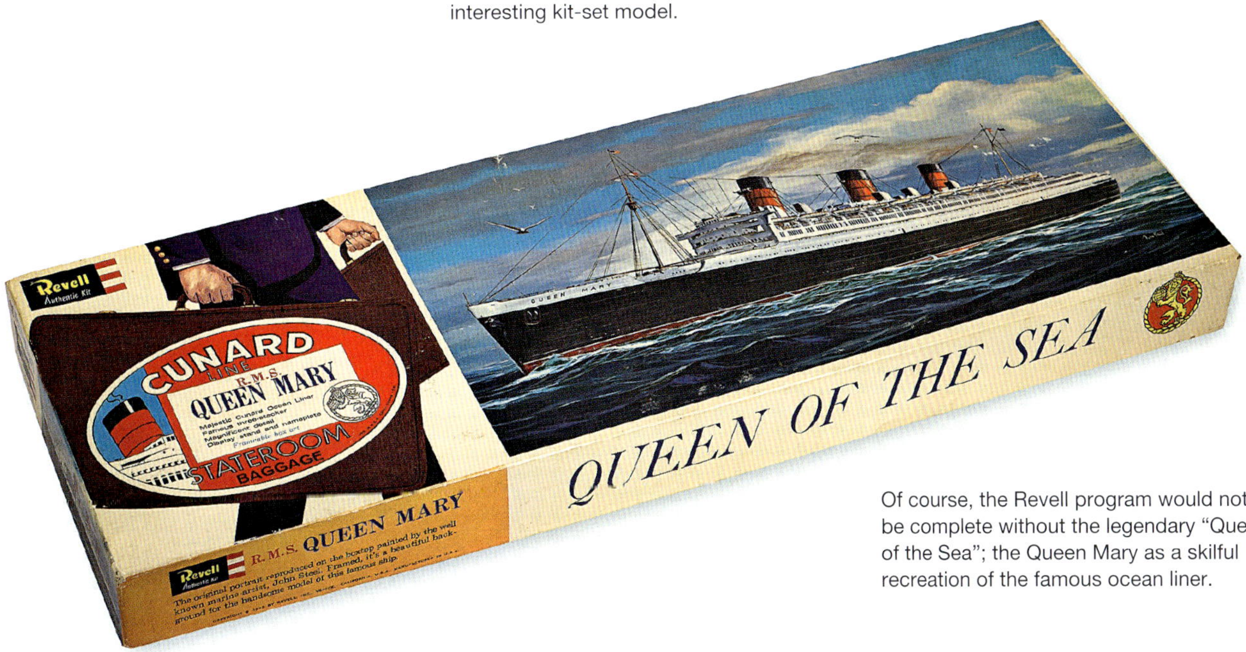

Of course, the Revell program would not be complete without the legendary "Queen of the Sea"; the Queen Mary as a skilful recreation of the famous ocean liner.

1963

In 1963, Revell USA introduces a new sector: Slot-car racers for the track debut in the scales of 1:24 and 1:32. Today, these kits are extremely hard to find.

On the title of this catalog, which was also printed in Bünde, the advertisers from East Westphalia showcased an important innovation that would turn into another long-term seller: the first civilian aircraft flying true-to-original Lufthansa colors: the Boeing 727 Europajet H-240. It was all but inevitable that this model would sell extremely well in Germany. The "race to the moon" was complemented by a space series with the Atlas launcher as well as the Mercury and Gemini model kits. Plastic kit models keenly followed the race to the moon that had been announced by President Kennedy. In a way, Revell wrote aerospace history in 1:X. The Bismarck and Tirpitz joined the range and for many years would also accompany the Revell fleet and ensure a stable turnover in the ship sector. Revell experimented, however, with new products such as a Cadet Series with automobile kits based on European vehicles in small, diverse scales of around 1:40. The first models were the Jaguar MK II, Volkswagen Beetle, Karmann Ghia, Ford Consul de Luxe, Vauxhall Cresta, Triumph TR 3 and the Rover 3 litre. German and English models set the pace at first. Small-scale Double Car Kits with American dragsters were also produced, including a limited run of very small-scale motorbikes. As a very unusual product, a weather station was also launched, most likely originating from a liaison with Kosmos. Today it is an extremely sought-after and valuable rarity. Finally, featured in the catalog for the first time was the new Revell car racetrack in the scales 1:32 (Corvette, Lola T-70, E-Type and Ferrari GTO) and 1:24 (Ford and Lotus Indianapolis). The vehicles and tracks, especially in top conditions, are in hot demand among collectors today. Particularly since the 1:24 models from Revell had extremely powerful motors. In the States, the larger slot-car racing dimensions yielded higher revenue right from the outset. One reason for was that American homes generally had more space to set up the racetrack. Over the next years, Revell USA continued to expand the range in both scales. The 1:24 and 1:32 models could also be purchased as a self-assembly kit.

Now in the new Revell dimension for compact aircraft kits in a 1:144-scale, Revell unveils the modern passenger Boeing 727 aircraft to the public – flying the colors of Lufthansa.

1964

Already in the mid-sixties, Revell adds another new theme with rocket miniatures.

Revell at Bünde opened the throttle even more with its own in-house catalogs. For the first time, the inside pages of the prospectus were printed in full color. The emphasis of the range was still on aircraft, particularly the 1:27-scale range of the so-called 600 Series. With this, Revell America slowly began to establish series in which models were kept to one construction size. Thus, it became increasingly more important for modelers, as it allowed for a better comparison between the different originals. With the 1:72 model, one-sixth of an inch on the model equated to a foot in length of the original. Moreover, there was also the relatively broad range of rockets and missile weapons. And in the ship sector, too, this year was mainly influenced by military types. The car segment still focused predominantly on American vehicles, with only a few European cars included in the range at this stage. After all, fans shouldn't forget: The VW Beetle and VW Karmann Ghia in 1:1 were selling extremely well in the States, as well. That said, models of British car marques also proved very popular with car buyers in America. A modest military series now became standard. New to the range were models of horses, a Palomino and Blaze King. With this, Revell made the first attempt to target girls. The fact that accessories took on an increasingly more important role at Revell was underlined by a small special product range Made by Humbrol, and this would be gradually expanded. With this, the managers recognized another growing market. Strangely, the 1964 catalog made no reference to the Revell slot-car racetrack. At that time there had been delays in the market launch. Aside from that, radio interference of the electric motors and controllers that were required in Germany caused additional problems. Nevertheless, Revell refused to give up on the sector, and instead withdrew this item from its 1964 catalog for technical reasons in order to make an even stronger comeback later.

The stallion Blaze King is not the only thing to spur Revell on in 1964. Animal models also become part of the range.

1965

The 1965 catalog highlights the automobile as a paragon of Revell products. The slot-car track is emblazoned on the title as its most important sales pillar.

With the return of the slot-car track after its omission from the previous year's catalog, the Revell catalog of 1965 made a mighty comeback. The fast racers were the stars on the 1965 title. Highlights in the range included models powered by electric motors, such as harbor tugs, the Oriana and sport fishing boats, all with a one-piece hull. The 1:72 Phantom enjoyed its premier and immediately became a top seller and would remain so for a long time. The first dragster, a typical American topic that was technically interesting but largely unknown in Germany, also made an appearance: As was the case with Revell's first big 1:8-scale motorbikes such as the Triumph Tiger in two versions. In the 1965 catalog, Revell presented for the first time a larger range of racetracks and expanded its involvement in this field. In the foreground were complete sets as well as individual vehicles and racing cars in the 1:32 and 1:24 scales. It was not common knowledge that Revell included figurines of the four Beatles, with all four making their debut in 1965. They were developed by Revell Inc in the USA and produced predominantly for the American market. Very few model kits made it to Europe and, in Germany, too, they were more of a secondary product. The license for the Fabulous Four was valid for just two years. Today, these model kits fetch eye-watering prices amongst collectors. During my first company tour at the beginning of December 1968, I noticed a 1:8-scale kit of Paul McCartney in an odds-and-ends shelf, which then became my first private purchase at Revell. The gross retail price at that time came to 6.75 DM. Oddly, the fact that Ringo Starr was never offered on the German market has never been explained. Over the years, I managed to acquire the other three Beatles figures, one in the USA (George), one in England (Ringo) and one (John) from a liquidation sale in Germany. The four hold a place of honor in my display cabinet. It's a shame that we'll probably never see a reissue of these four due to licensing difficulties. Had this been the case they would definitely have attracted a great deal of attention.

With the now established 1:72 aircraft scale, the navy version of the new Phantom II makes its debut for the "kit king" in 1965 and is clearly one of the most popular kits.

1966

Revell's racetrack range causes a furor, hence Revell strengthens its market position here in 1966 with the Gran Turismo Racing Set.

The 1:72-scale slowly emerged as the dimension that Revell preferred to offer in its aircraft sector. And this was reflected very clearly in the 1966 catalog. Revell even successfully added four-engine bomber planes from the Second World War for the first time with the B-17, Liberator, Lancaster and FW 200, and these, too, boosted the 1:72 scale. The motorbike line that Revell had launched the previous year was continued in 1966. For the first time, the Americans miniaturized a Honda, the CB 72 Super Sport. Motorcycles in a variety of dimensions would accompany Revell over the next decades. In America, the range of Harley-Davidsons had proven extremely popular, so in addition to the established Japanese motorbikes, Revell also added German and Italian brands to its two-wheel program. In fact, it was in the mid-sixties when Revell discovered a completely new theme with motorbikes that worked extremely well. However, since there was a great deal of technology to reproduce, the elaborate kits proved rather expensive and more suited to advanced modelers. In close cooperation with Humbrol, the company steadily continued to expand its accessories program, which was also featured in the 1966 catalog. In the slot-car segment, accessories played an increasingly important role. Revell followed closely what was happening successfully with real race cars on the world's circuits: tweaking. It was only given the name 'tuning' much later in the times of AMG and Co. However, in 1966, customizing meant that Revell was able to offer a wide range of axle drives, pinions, engines and especially tires, which would aid the specific vehicle setups to suit individual racetracks and, of course, make the cars faster. Moreover, in the slot-car program, one couldn't ignore the spare parts business. Ambitious slot-car enthusiasts who were keen to compete with their mini-racers on the tracks usually had an enormous need for spare parts, which, of course, the factory was happy to provide. This was certainly a market that the Revell managers did not want to miss out on.

Revell's program from 1966 ranges from the new Avro Lancaster as a 1:72 plastic kit through to an experiment set, which thanks to a small weather station could make forecasts.

1967

A major change was clearly visible on the title of the 1967 catalog: The Revell logo had switched from the black and yellow lettering on the Authentic Kits to the now well-known but still black and yellow "Revell" logo. Revell had literally made itself a name and this should be reflected in the new logo. Once again, aircraft became the high-fliers in the program, thus the selection in 1967 expanded significantly. In this regard, the Vietnam War left its first marks on the miniatures. An entire series of airplane and helicopter models were based on those used in that war. Revell made history with its model kits. And if wars like the one in Vietnam were part of that history, then this would be reflected in the products. Wars are made my people, not Revell. In 1967, vehicle model kits were offered on a scale of 1:32 and with a new level of detailing. The latest 'big' vehicle program began with the Messerschmitt Me 109, a Supermarine Spitfire, the Curtiss P-40, and, in keeping with the Vietnam theme, a Bell UH-1 D as well as a Bell Cobra. However, by 1967 it was not yet clear that the 1:32-scale would become another huge international benchmark for Revell's model airplanes. Following the Gemini program, the Americans launched the Apollo program, thus Revell, too, immediately pushed the appropriate kit set in the scales 1:96 and 1:48 onto the launch pad at Cape Canaveral. Man was on his way to the moon and Revell would definitely be alongside, in hundreds of thousands of children's rooms around the world. The vehicle category, however, suffered a setback in Germany, which was undoubtedly due to the lack of interest in American cars. Although German automobiles had enjoyed world fame for years, Revell had pushed this topic to one side. Nevertheless, all hell broke loose on the highways in the motorbike scene with Revell bringing a Honda Scrambler and a Honda Racing bike in the 1:8-scale. With this, the two-wheel motorcycles kept the throttle open at Revell.

Revell produces interesting model kits for everything that points to the future in terms of technology: Such as the concept of the Supersonic Clipper, which heralds the arrival of the Concorde.

In Germany, Heinz-Georg Schöneberg throws himself into promoting the Revell brand. In this regard, city championships for slot-car racing should help. The response from the public is certainly very convincing.

In addition, Revell now builds a small world around its kits, as underlined by the F-102A Delta Dagger kit, which includes an impressive range of airfield accessories and even figures for aircraft modelers and thus takes on a whole new dimension.

1968

Public relations – and Revell is no exception. The photo shows a group of visitors in the computing (today IT) department at the Vedes firm with Ulli Taubert and PA Hiltrud Schöneberg.

Ulli Taubert, the author of this chronicle, joined Revell in the eventful year of 1968. This was the big year for student movements and the hippie culture. Bad news such as the assassinations of Martin Luther King and Robert F. Kennedy spread around the world. The new value added tax was set at ten percent, bathing regulations were relaxed in Passau/ Germany and women were now permitted to wear bikinis in outdoor pools. In the summer of 1968, the Prague Spring was brutally crushed through the invasion of the Warsaw Pact countries. Protests against everything conservative flowed out into the streets, and still today we talk with great pride of the '68ers. On a completely different front, this year heralded changes in the German school system. Easter had always marked the end of the school year, however, a switch to summer was announced in 1968. Negative side effects included the transitional shorter school year, which also affected Taubert. In order to follow his dream and study business administration, he first needed to complete his education. However, the Bünde firm had already chosen their apprentices at Easter, which put Taubert in a tricky situation. But at this point serendipity stepped in: Taubert had grown up very close to the RAF Airport in Gütersloh, which piqued his interest in aircraft, especially those of the Royal Air Force. In mid-1964, the Taubert family moved to the town of Südlengern not far from Bünde, where the East Westphalian met

In 1968, as well, Revell likes to fly high with its new airplane model kits. The DC-8 Jetliner makes its debut sporting the livery of Sweden's SAS.

Space travel continues to skyrocket at Revell: Illustrated here is the Apollo spaceship as a 1:96-scale model.

his first girlfriend. Her name was Ingrid. This would be an encounter that would play an important role in his life and at Revell. A neighbor in his home of Südlengern knew someone who needed an apprentice. The neighbor was a building contractor, his acquaintance was a general manager, both of the gentlemen were members of the Bünde Shooting Club. The company turned out to be Revell. Taubert had heard about the model kit manufacturer at the age of six, but he knew it as an American company, hence this Revell must be something entirely different. Nevertheless, Taubert went to Bünde for an interview. When the large door to the entrance swung open, he immediately spotted the giant wall paintings of the Santa Maria and Boeing 707, with the massive Revell logo above. He was over the moon. His interview with Heinz-Georg Schöneberg in a room thick with cigar smoke concluded with the managing director taking a look at Taubert's somewhat mediocre school report. His comment: "Oh well, it's not particularly grand but let's give you a go anyway." The trial turned into fifty years. When Taubert joined the firm on December 1, 1968, the company was still relatively small with a staff of just 35. At his place of work in a former cigar shop located in the Bünde town center, Taubert was shown the ropes by the former head of purchasing and eventual managing director and CEO, Kurt Haubrok. The tour of the premises finished after ten minutes, that's how small the firm was at that time. During the tour, Taubert spied a Beatles model kit, and this became his first private acquisition. We're talking about the Apollo era, when the tests for the planned moon landing were in full swing. Sales of each and every product in this segment went sky high and stayed there. This was also the time when the interest in slot-car racing began to wane. More and more competitors were popping up, all offering considerably cheaper models; prices which Revell America couldn't match for its products at the exchange rate at that time of 3.65 DM.

1969

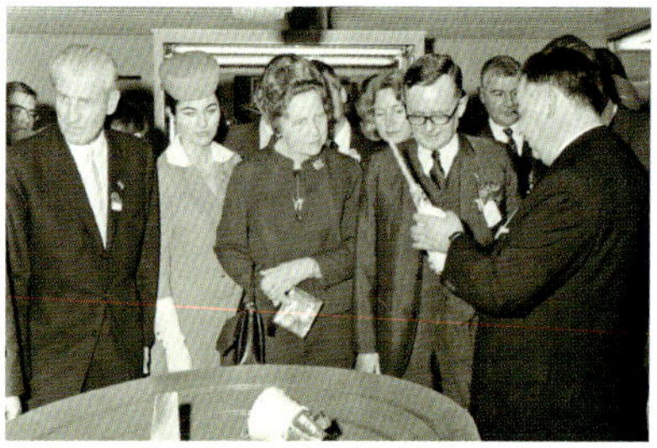

An honor for Revell: In 1969, the Federal Minister of Economic Affairs Karl Schiller visited the East Westphalians at their generously dimensioned stand at the internationally renowned toy fair in Nuremberg, Franconia – a real feather in their cap.

The model year started with a bang: In the previous years, Revell had brought tools to Bünde in order to produce on site and to avoid the extremely expensive US imports. Starting out as a low volume operation then turned into series production by the end of 1968. Due to significantly cheaper manufacturing costs from two Bünde-based partner companies – Balda and Brockfeld & Meier – Revell Germany managed to reduce prices drastically in time for the 1969 toy fair. This paved the way for an increase in sales, and this trend would continue for years. The new catalog was characterized by further "typically German" models, all of which were created in-house, such as the Starfighter, Boeing 707 Lufthansa and Z-1 Destroyer. The Vietnam series was expanded. Joining the motorbike range was the 1:8 Harley Davidson Electra Glide, which would eventually turn into a long-standing seller. During this year, Revell sold off the remaining racetrack series. Already at this time, the model kit manufacturer was searching for new mainstays and entered into a cooperation with the Danish company Bilo from Bramdrupdam: High-quality wooden toys for pre-school and kindergarten children, all in the upper price segment. Unsurprisingly, the best Revell product from this special year was the Apollo Saturn V from the Apollo program, the large 1:96-scale rocket. Following is one of the many anecdotes on this subject: Revell had made agreements with the

There are certain models that run like a common thread through the model range of Revell. The Bismarck is definitely one of them. This battleship first appeared in 1963 in the catalog of the specialists from the United States as a plastic model kit.

Brand new in Revell's range of model kits is the Triumph Custom Show Bike, which would give the brand's motorcycle line a whole new impetus. Custom bikes and show cars were extremely trendy in America at this time.

department store chains Karstadt, Hertie and Kaufhof to position so-called *propaganden*, or special demo staff, in these stores during the Christmas period. For this purpose, Revell hired salespeople for a limited time who sold articles on commission in selected department stores from the beginning of October until Christmas. At their stands they had a display case with pre-assembled models that were the same in every store. Of course, all of the stores wanted articles from the Apollo line, including the Saturn V. For these display cases, it was no problem to build the smaller models, but the larger models were a problem, because 80 of them had to be assembled from early February to late September in time for the Nuremberg toy fair. Taubert offered to take over the job himself and he succeeded. For this, the young apprentice had to empty his entire attic to accommodate all the models. Even today, the specialist can assemble this model virtually with his eyes closed. And since building Revell's models was a paid job, of course, the youngster earned enough money to buy himself his first motorbike, a 250 cc Yamaha.

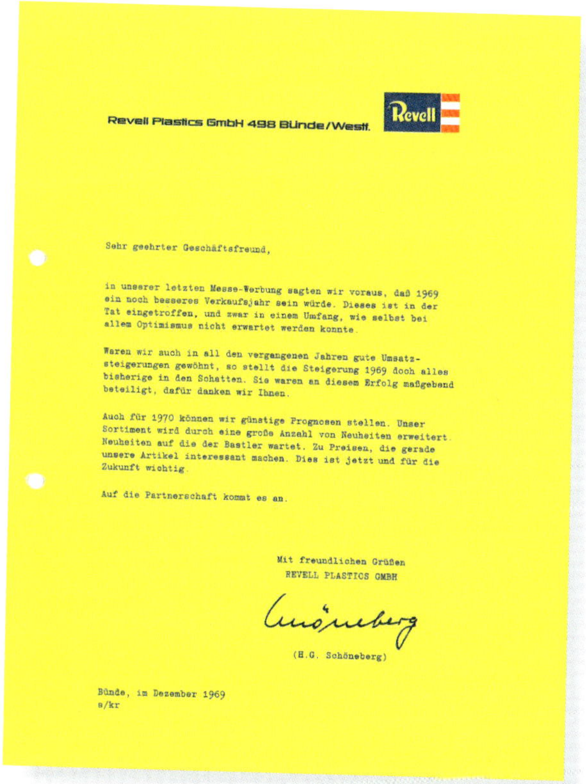
Revell Plastics GmbH 498 Bünde/Westf.

Revell

Sehr geehrter Geschäftsfreund,

in unserer letzten Messe-Werbung sagten wir voraus, daß 1969 ein noch besseres Verkaufsjahr sein würde. Dieses ist in der Tat eingetroffen, und zwar in einem Umfang, wie selbst bei allem Optimismus nicht erwartet werden konnte.

Waren wir auch in all den vergangenen Jahren gute Umsatzsteigerungen gewöhnt, so stellt die Steigerung 1969 doch alles bisherige in den Schatten. Sie waren an diesem Erfolg maßgebend beteiligt, dafür danken wir Ihnen.

Auch für 1970 können wir günstige Prognosen stellen. Unser Sortiment wird durch eine große Anzahl von Neuheiten erweitert. Neuheiten auf die der Bastler wartet. Zu Preisen, die gerade unsere Artikel interessant machen. Dies ist jetzt und für die Zukunft wichtig.

Auf die Partnerschaft kommt es an.

Mit freundlichen Grüßen
REVELL PLASTICS GMBH

(H.G. Schöneberg)

Bünde, im Dezember 1969
s/kr

In a bright yellow circular, Revell boss Heinz-Georg Schöneberg announces to the business partners that Revell has once again enjoyed a record year in 1969.

1970

At the 1970 trade fair party, managing director Heinz-Georg Schöneberg welcomes a "real" astronaut as a guest of honor. The car range expands with the EMPI imp dune buggy in scales of 1:32 and 1:25.

The turnover of the company boomed so drastically that the Revell premises in the Bünde town center literally burst at the seams. This year, the successful East Westphalians had leased no fewer than 36 warehouses in and around Bünde, from garages to an entire hall. The decision to create its own premises, to build in other words, seemed completely logical.

This year also proved to be an enjoyable one for Ulli Taubert. Although he was just an apprentice, he was allowed to attend the trade fair at Nuremberg for the first time. The only problem was his hair length and rather wild beard. Both were not in keeping for "a German salesman at a trade fair stand." The apprentice was given a choice: trade fair or hair. Despite some people getting upset by this, he chose the fair – after all, this was a once in a lifetime chance and his hair would grow back. This was a game that Taubert would play with his boss, "Uncle Schöneberg" (as he was nicknamed by his staff), every year until his retirement from the business. The fair itself, of course, was dominated by the Americans' successful moon landing. For the exhibition, Revell had organized an original astronaut suit from the Apollo mission from NASA. This outfit had to be worn for the entire duration of the fair by the then distribution manager Heinz Jeike. He definitely lost a lot of sweat and weight in Nuremberg that year.

The new Revell catalog presented a raft of novelties, particularly in the area of 1:32-scale aircraft, including a P-38 Lightning and 1:8-scale motorbikes such as the Kawasaki Mach III. The catalog dedicated four pages to the space program alone. Another sensation back then was the Disney license for *Herbie, the Love Bug*, which proved to be a big seller for Revell in the scale of 1:25. Another top seller debuted this year: the Gorch Fock. Revell created the tall ship from the existing USS Eagle, with defiant mercilessness and without changing the shape at all. And then there was the wife of "Uncle Lew", Royle Glaser. Totally unsuited to the role of boss, she attempted to introduce new and peculiar ideas every year – borderline ideas that Revell then had to sell. In 1970 it was the 3D Yarn-Art project: printed self-adhesive films that were glued with colored yarns to create a motif. Girls and women were the target group, and, of course, we tried everything to make such a product appeal to the market. But the flight to the moon eclipsed everything and was definitely easier to sell.

1971

Finished in felt and in an oval frame, Donald Duck salutes fans in 1971 in a different type of Revell kit.

The new company complex built the previous year in the new industrial area of Bünde-Ennigloh soon turned out to be too small, hence an expansion and the company's own production facility were planned. A sketch of the new warehouse and administration building was already illustrated in the new Revell catalog, signalizing a mood of optimism. The program itself grew exponentially, with one kit after the other offered, with tailor-made products for the German market such as a German Air Force Phantom and a Bundeswehr version of the UH-1 D proving especially popular. Another milestone was waiting in the wings: Revell Germany got the green light from the Revell Inc. mother company to produce its first in-house development. And because the motorcycle category was running at high revs at this time and BMW had just unleashed a new boxer generation, the team in Bünde decided to design this new BMW as a model kit themselves. Since we had no development department at Bünde, the head of advertising Heiner-Michael Hoffmann was given the job of contacting BMW and to include their relevant designer Hans Muth in the new motorbike program. Although Hans Muth wasn't responsible for the BMW/5-series, he was, however, the father of the R 90 S. Thanks to him, Revell received the documentation. We also got an original on loan for a few days from a BMW car dealer so that we could do our research. Since Heiner Hoffmann had no interest at all in motorbikes, the avid biker Ulli Taubert was approached and asked if he would like to work on the project. No sooner said than done. Taubert helped with the necessary work such as measuring, photographing, making notes, establishing model details and much more. Don't forget, this was completely new territory for Revell Germany. Everything then went to the mold manufacturers in Portugal as a dossier for the product. This partner not only had Revell in Bünde as a customer but also the sister company Revell (GB) in Potters Bar, which had also been founded in 1956 and was responsible for the development and production in Europe. A year later, the boxer-BMW appeared in the catalog for the first time.

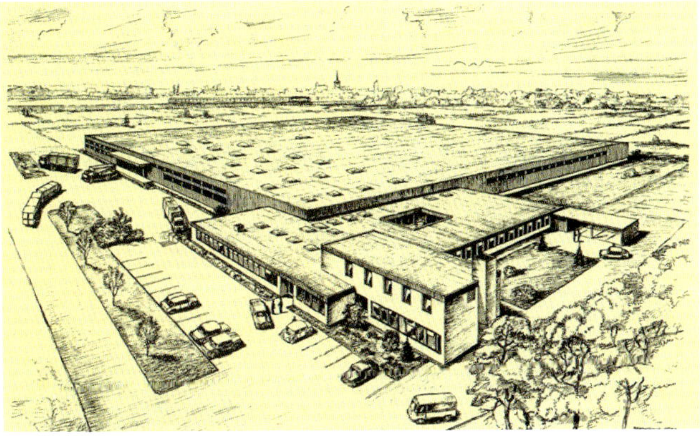

In contrast, Heinz-Georg Schöneberg diligently builds on the future of Revell in Bünde, as outlined in this sketch.

Snap Fit is the name of a new 1:32-scale model kit. The Beetle can be assembled without glue. A model, incidentally, that Revell recently revised and offered again to customers as a new edition.

Here is an anecdote that proved critical for the later work of the developer Ulli Taubert: With his apprenticeship coming to an end on October 1, 1971, he received a college offer at the HWF in Bielefeld, where he wanted to study business administration. While working on the original BMW R 75/5, he realized that he had to own one of these motorbikes. After the final work on the original, he in fact did buy the 750-cc BMW. The story continues: On 31 July, Taubert reconnected with Ingrid, his childhood sweetheart mentioned earlier. And since she was a motorbike enthusiast, the two made plans to meet up the next day for a ride to grab a coffee at Gütersloh. With sunshine and a temperature of 30-degrees Celsius, the weather was perfect for a little jaunt. In Gütersloh, the pair was involved in a bad accident when a Beetle shunted them from the road. Ingrid and Ulli ended up in hospital with serious injuries, with Taubert spending the rest of the year there. The upshot of all this: the college position was gone. After his discharge from hospital, Taubert had a word to the boss to ask whether he could continue working at Revell to bridge the two-year waiting period for another university spot. The answer was yes, and that bridging period turned into 50 years. Revell and Taubert have Ingrid to thank for this indirectly, without whom this situation would never have arisen. In spite of all the pain, Taubert was and still is very grateful. Many wonderful, exciting and adventurous years as a model developer at Revell would follow.

Tailor-made versions of the model kit gain in popularity. Revell's Phantom II kit, for example, is launched in the German Air Force version and also receives the matching decals.

1972

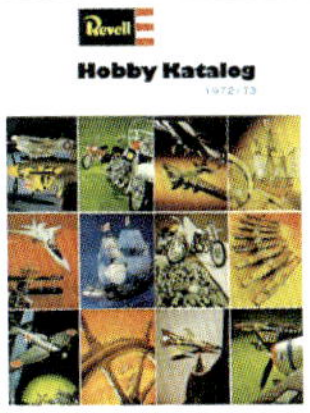

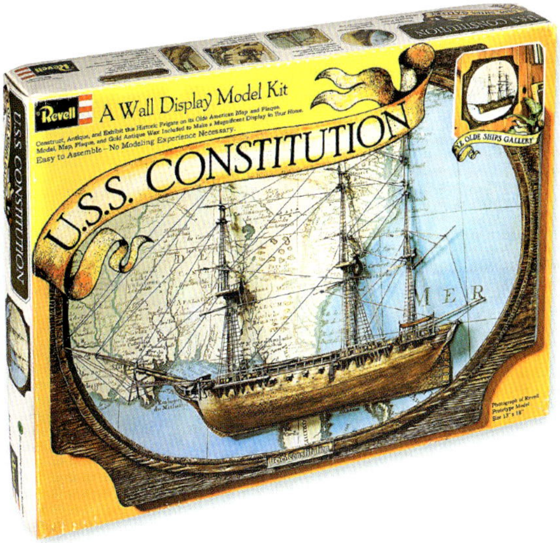

Revell sets its sails: The plastic model kit of the USS Constitution turns into a top seller amongst fans.

The boom in plastic model kits continued, steadily supplemented by typical German products, such as the Boeing 707 "Luftwaffe" and a DC-10 in Lufthansa colors. An F-4 Phantom was added to the still large 1:32-scale aircraft segment. The Apollo/Eagle program was still on an upward trajectory. And the strong motorbike category was complemented by 1:8 trikes and a new, compact series of 1:12-scale bikes. The Japanese Tamiya Corporation also focused on this small-scale model. Our American boss, Royle Glaser, again hit on a great idea, the so-called Broadside models, in which half sailing ships were glued on to a background with historical nautical charts. The series started with three motives, which – as difficult as it was for experts to believe – enjoyed little success. Parallel to this, Mrs Glaser's 3D Yarn-Art was now offered as a wall decoration and with Disney licenses. Revell had considered making an additional use out of the partly very attractive packaging illustrations. During this time, jigsaw puzzles were very popular, so Revell Deutschland pieced together puzzles with its own illustrations and launched them on the market. Initially, six different motives with 280 puzzle pieces and six others with 500 pieces were offered. For years, these puzzles enjoyed great success, with healthy sales at very little outlay – and production on the doorstep in Kirchlengern.

The year was overshadowed by the death of the Revell founder Lewis H. Glaser on September 12, 1972, after a long fight with cancer. The sole heiress was his wife Royle Glaser, who had already been managing the operative side of the company since 1970.

Ulli Taubert was in his bridging time, moving from one department to the other, which ultimately gave him little motivation. Taubert eventually applied for an outside job. Just before signing the contract for the new job – back then with the Yamaha importer Mitsui Deutschland – he had to return to the hospital to have the metal screws that had held him together after the accident removed from his body. While there, he was visited by two friendly colleagues, Richard Breves and Ulla Montua, who offered him a position to help build a completely new export department at Revell. This, of course, piqued young Taubert's interest and he immediately accepted the offer. A close friendship still connects them all today and a fabulous success story unfolded.

In 1972, the first in-house development of Revell in Bünde causes a sensation: the BMW R75/5 in the scale of 1:8.

1973

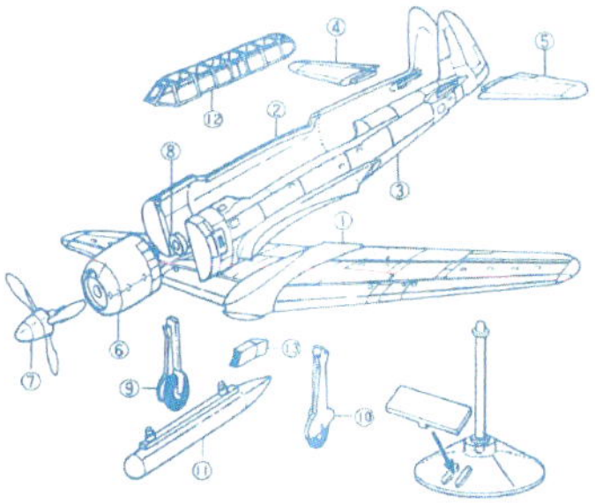

The exploded-view drawings of the Revell kits are becoming increasingly more elaborate (left) and the managing director Heinz-Georg Schöneberg takes center stage on the title of the renowned specialist magazine *Spielzeug-Markt*.

This year was busy with the planning and the start of construction of the company's own production facility. Since producing in Germany made sense due to the unfavorable exchange rate, Revell invested heavily. The project consisted of an additional new 5,000-square-meter building right next to the main building. The catalog showed a photo of the existing 12,000-square-meter building for its own headquarters in East Westphalia. The catalog also featured new products in the plastic model kit range, with the focus on a new 1:144 mini-series, starting with aircraft and the large-scale 1:32 aircraft, which now included a fleet of 30 different types. Moreover, new sailing ships and so-called Top Fuel Dragsters in a scale of 1:16 enhanced the range. The latter theme came from America. Revell Germany also expanded its jigsaw puzzle kits. Moreover, Revell increased its own product line, offering brushes and glue, thus making itself less dependent on Humbrol supplies. And let's not forget the motorcycle program in the scales 1:8 and 1:12, which now encompassed 25 models. As a special mission, the East Westphalians sent a police version of its proven BMW 75/5 out on patrol. Revell used good old-fashioned research and sent Ulli Taubert to call on members of the local police force in Bünde for help. This would benefit the look of the eventual kit hugely, with the kit pieces lovingly realized. A lucky coincidence: The local force had just added a BMW-boxer to its fleet of service vehicles. In addition to the usual detailed images and measurements, a photo of the original was also needed for the title of the box. This shooting took place at the A30 autobahn from Bad Oeynhausen towards Amsterdam. The autobahn at that time was not yet open for everyday traffic, which certainly helped when taking the photos. Ulli Taubert: "We positioned the Bünde police motorbike with a driver on the motorway, placed a truck from our railway agent in front and took photos. That's how the box title was created, showing the policeman in the outfit of that era. Those days it was a relatively simple way to create a package title, you can't compare it to the effort needed today."

At Revell Germany the focus shifted to internationalization. Initially, the East Westphalians exported to BeNeLux, France and Italy. There was, after all, a stipulation from the USA that Bünde would only export to the EEC countries, and the British branch in Potters Bar would be responsible for the EFTA countries. Theoretically. Taubert recalls: "Back then we did occasional business in poly-bags with the national importer of Yugoslavia, at that time the first and only customer in the 'Eastern Bloc'."

Revell proves inventive and comes up with a jigsaw puzzle of the Gorch Fock. The legendary BMW-boxer makes its debut in 1973, now as a patrol bike for the German Federal Police in a scale of 1:8.

Revell in Bünde grows and thrives. In a newly developed industrial area, there is now more space for the steady expansion of the creative and successful East Westphalian company.

Managing director Schöneberg discusses the future strategies with the founder's widow, Royle Glaser. This is no easy task, as the relationship between the USA and Bünde becomes more and more challenging.

1974

Japanese motorcycles move into the limelight. At Revell, the Kawasaki Mach III debuts as a plastic kit in the large 1:12 scale with very fine detailing.

The excitement of this year was not so much about new products but more so to do with Revell's export activities. In 1974, the company used its own sales team for the first time ever for an export country: in the Netherlands, which had just been defeated 1:2 by the Federal Republic of German in the Munich final of the Football World Cup. For Revell, this signified a huge move in terms of expansion. Over the years, Holland had become Revell's most important export country over the years, and this would also have an impact on the ongoing product development. Revell's export department set up a separate Dutch department with Ton Lourier and Bert De Vries as employees. 1974, however, was also characterized by another important setting of strategic directions. First of all, it marked the start of a cooperation with Esci and Italaerei, both from Bologna in Italy. Italaerei had been founded in 1962 by two friends, Giuliano Malservisi and Pietro Parmeggiani. The pair was not particularly inspired by the model kits on the market, so they decided to set up their own line in the early seventies. Italaerei, which would later change to Italeri, initially introduced just the 1:72 aircraft from the Second World War as well as 1:35-scale military vehicles from the same era. Esci was originally founded in 1930 but only began producing plastic model kits in 1972 under Dino Coppola. At that time, Esci only manufactured military products in the scale of 1:72 as well as 1:9-scale motorbikes. Both companies grew significantly and expanded their range to include other segments. For years, Revell was their biggest buyer. The association that began back then continues to the present day. Revell had always had positive experiences with Humbrol, however the market leader of model kits in Germany decided to break away and create its own paint assortment. This decision was made in 1974. Last but not least, the inauguration of the company's new in-house production plant at Bünde was scheduled for this year, marking another step towards independence and cost-optimization for the East Westphalians. For this reason, the only in-house development to come out of Revell Germany this year was a racing version of the very successful BMW R 75/5 line. A version that the Bünde team virtually created themselves sporting a Labitzke race-bodywork: dyed-in-the-wool motorbike freaks knew what this means.

But the traditional range of ships with the U-47 and the Boeing 747 "Lufthansa" are not neglected at Revell.

1975

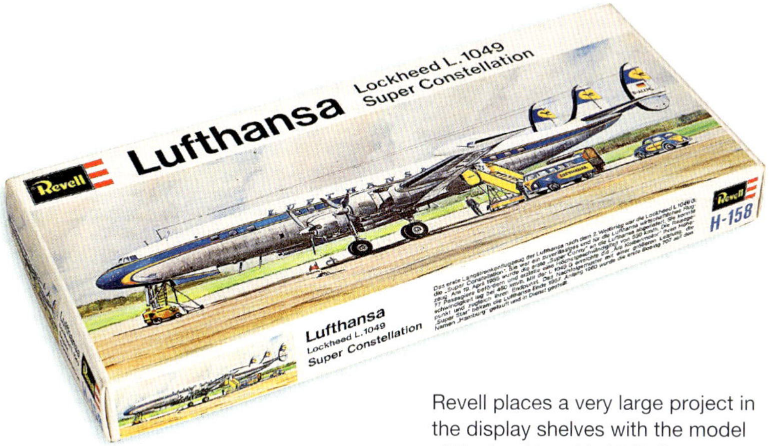

Revell places a very large project in the display shelves with the model of the Lockheed L-1049 Super Constellation in the scale 1:144.

Revell's new building activities were also highlighted in the 1975 catalog: The latest edition showed a photo montage of the entire Revell complex after the last of the planned expansion stages. In terms of new developments, the Bünde team concentrated on one strategic novelty. In the meantime, a German Air Force version of the 1:32-scale Phantom was refined for the domestic craft market. Revell had tweaked the popular aircraft in line with a real version of the Luftwaffe Phantom. This modified kit now included special components that made it possible to build a Phantom F-4F. Up until this point, Revell Germany had stuck with new decals, but had let the typical detailing of the Luftwaffe version slide. This changed with the Phantom. In addition to decals, essential components were changed. Thus, this kit was one of the first authentic German conversion models in the program and a benchmark for future versions and new developments. With this, Revell Germany embarked on a new strategy to further distinguish itself from the growing competition in the plastic model-making arena. Making its debut in the 1975 catalog was an S-55 Helicopter in the colors of the German Rescue Air Force (DRF) and a Super Constellation took off with true-to-original Lufthansa decor. Still enjoying very strong sales was the aircraft range in the large-scale 1:32, which Revell had established internationally. Italeri and Esci expanded their range significantly, resulting in the German model kit market leader from Bünde also recording enormous sales growth. Revell gave the small aircraft model kits a facelift. The 1:72-scale models were now renamed "3 in 1". This meant that decals for three different variants were now included in every kit of this new series. This product would continue through the program in the coming decades.

For model shipbuilders, Revell reintroduces its USS Olympia in 1975 as a 1:240-scale plastic model kit.

1976

In the now established 1:72-scale, Revell surprises with the General Dynamics F-16A including a separate engine on a provided delivery van.

New developments once again stood at the forefront at Revell during this year. In almost all product areas, the East Westphalians expanded their program with interesting new releases. In the year 1976, 20 years after the founding of Revell Germany, several products made their debut and would eventually become standard articles in the program. Among them was the Mirage III in a scale of 1:72, the SR-71 in the same dimension and, as a top newcomer, the F-16 following the 1972 model year, the sales figure of which would amount to hundreds of thousands over the course of time – a real best-seller. This year, a new ship also hit the market, the Titanic in 1:570-scale, and would remain part of the program and is still offered today. Moreover, the export department expanded its activities in the Netherlands with special Dutch products. The first novelty that Revell brought to the market from this range was a Boeing 747 featuring an authentic KLM livery. The development department had to restrict itself to original photos of the KLM aircraft, as the new version could only be realized with decals. Special components were not yet necessary here. Revell also made a special deal in 1976, buying all the tools from Casadio in Italy. Their Snap-Fit-style mini-ship series in the 1:1200-scale is still sold today. In terms of its technological development, Revell accompanied this series from start to finish. This meant in-house production, in-house packaging, in-house decals. Revell Germany took over the exclusive worldwide distribution from another company with completely new products: Tris Models from Trieste in Italy. Their specialty was model kits made of wood, with outstanding detailing and individual components. Revell then sold these very successfully for some years. Because the deal had been done quite quickly, a separate brochure had to be printed that first year to showcase the new products. The existing cooperation with Esci and Italeri had reached such a point that the current Revell catalog had a total of 128 pages in order to present all the products clearly. Both companies contributed greatly to the wave of novelties. This year also proved crucial for the accessories sector. Revell immediately discontinued the distribution of the long-selling Humbrol colors and instead introduced its own complete color palette developed and produced by a paint manufacturer not far from Bünde. At the same time, the in-house accessory range expanded with products such as craft knives, thinners, hobby kits, as well as tube and liquid adhesives.

The Netherlands gains in importance. Hence, Revell's model fleet now includes the Jumbo 747 in 1:144, flying the colors of KLM.

One catalog is almost not enough. For this reason, separate brochures are printed specifically for wooden boats and mini-ships.

1977

Partnerships with the likes of Esci and Italeri contribute to rapid expansion of Revell's model range, opening up successful core brands and new target groups.

This year's Revell catalog had an impressive 162 pages, an edition that set a clear record. The new product range this year was characterized by American developments, with the assistance in some cases of the Bünde team. In view of incredibly strong business in the Netherlands, two products that were developed completely in-house at Revell Germany were also included in the hefty catalog: the first was the incredibly successful version of the 1:72-scale F-16 model, unveiled for the first time in 1976 in the color of the Royal Netherlands Air Force (KLU). For this, the experts from Bünde assembled a ready-made model and placed it in front of the KLU airport in Leeuwarden for the photo shoot. Additional photos were shot in Leeuwarden to produce the image for the box. Another typical Dutch project was the version of the DC-10 in KLM colors. The liaison with KLM had begun the previous year, and this collaboration would continue successfully for many years to come. Another new product also celebrated its debut in 1977, this time developed by our American parent company: the Calypso, which was created at the time through a personal contact with Jacques Cousteau. The U.S. also contributed the Goodyear Blimp, an airship used for advertising purposes, which the hobbyists could recreate as models. Revell also put the first aircraft in the new 1:48-scale on the runway, and the 1:25 car category received a huge boost with the addition of new vehicle types. The Italaeri and Esci range also contributed new developments. Revell once again expanded its color and accessory range considerably. This year marked the debut of Revell's spray guns, with the Sprite created in conjunction with the company Badger, a specialist for such products. The absolute highlight of this year, however, was the purchase of the Radio Control division from the liquidation sale of Schuco. Model-making products for the RC area came onto the market under the name Hegi. The kits under this brand were showcased in a separate 36-page catalog. The inventory, machines and materials were transported from Allersberg near Nuremberg to Bünde, and moved into a new and separate building right next to the Revell headquarters. The personnel, from the division manager to the sales and development manager, were also taken on, with the staff relocating from Franconia to East Westphalia.

With Jacques-Yves Cousteau's Calypso, Revell sets out on a grand voyage of discovery in 1977.

1978

Revell's Rolls-Royce Phantom II in 1:16 scale visits the Mercedes Museum (right) and below is the model kit in the look of that time.

The management increased the number of pages in the complete catalog again this year, so the volume grew to 194 pages for the main catalog and another 110 pages for the *Funktionsmodellbau* catalog. The title was one big advertisement for a new top product, the 1:144 Space Shuttle that has remained unchanged in Revell's program until today. The Electronic Action Kits enhanced the range and the series of Dutch products further expanded the marketing. The main focus at that time was on exports and for me as a product developer this had top priority. The automobile area experienced a renaissance, including the large scale models. The cooperation with Italeri reached a whole new level with the new Bo-105 (1:32) and with Esci's Porsche 934 and BMW 320 Turbo (1:24). But Hegi was the big hit of this year, with its own catalog advertising the assortment and a comprehensive accessory program. Taubert had nothing to do with this line of products, as Revell and Hegi were kept separate, even the premises. As the export manager for internal sales, I was involved in all international versions for our markets. This also included posters, stickers, t-shirts and much more, which we needed for our work in the Netherlands at that time, and so we were a nose ahead of the domestic market, at least technically.

In addition to automobiles, the Space Shuttle Enterprise including the Spacelab (left) belong to the undisputed top news of Revell's 1978 catalog.

1979

The Discovery Shuttle 1:72-scale model kit from Revell (left and bottom right the 1979 catalog layout) continues the space series with great success.

On this year's catalog title, buyers immediately recognized the dominating influence of Revell USA and Revell Great Britain. After the departure of the managing director, Heinz-Georg Schöneberg, who in the truest sense of the word had become independent with the Hegi range, Kurt Haubrok and Colin Dunne took over the controls at the main center. Kurt Haubrok was responsible for the technical side of things, with Colin Dunne taking care of the commercial aspects. Parallel to this, the long-standing cooperation with Italeri came to an end, with the new management offering all Esci products in a separate catalog. Strategists expanded the exceptionally successful Electronic Action Kits. The shuttle range grew by two more items, including a large 1:72 version. Other special items for the Dutch market also rolled of the assembly line. Another long-time seller dropped anchor at Revell: the Ghost Ship. Otherwise, the program, especially the newcomers, consisted of products that were mainly important for the U.S. market. This model year also marked the start of the conversion to the four-digit article number system, after the old system became too limiting and inflexible. I wasn't that involved with developments, but in addition to my job as an export office manager I picked up another responsibility in marketing services, which was nothing more than a detailed forecasting system in order to better control production planning in the future.

Flying the colors of the Royal Netherlands Air Force (left), the 1:72-scale F-16 makes its debut.

Things can sometimes get a bit scary at Revell. The glow-in-the-dark 1:72 Pirate Ghost Ship proves this.

The General Dynamics F-16A model is now offered as a plastic kit in a large 1:32-scale.

1980

This year, the European program again had a distinctive American influence, with the business commercial director Colin Dunne following the US requirements as if they were a master plan. It started at the height of the "snap" product time; model kits that were assembled without using glue. As the name suggests, the parts simply snapped together thanks to cleverly-made fasteners. The catalog alone, which I personally found to be one of the worst in Revell history, had our regular customers astonished at best, but more often shaking their heads. The entire catalog was done in England, from the design to the content. This catalog, however, was to cover both branches, Revell Plastics GmbH in Bünde and Revell (GB) Limited in Potters Bar. This time, the producers of the catalog often used rather plain model images and packaging, which made our products look very unappealing. The worst new aspect, however, was the format, not only was it bigger than A4, the entire thing was printed in landscape format. It was completely futile for us to protest. We were still regarded as the little Teutonic town with brave warriors. I don't want to say too much about the content, except that we still at least tried to do something good and appropriate for specific countries, for the German and Dutch markets, of course. Something typical of America: the rear section of the catalog included a long register of all the licenses, all listed separately. Licenses, now that's a topic that still turns hair gray at Revell. And it was in 1980 that these woes began.

The VW Beetle, especially as a convertible, is the star in the USA and Germany. For this reason, Revell builds it in a 1:25 scale from 1980.

Revell also enjoys making incredible flying kits and did it with a special kind of humor.

The Porsche Turbo Targa as a Snap Together kit in a 1:25-scale and the Porsche 928 in the large 1:16 scale expand Revell's fleet of sporty cars.

1981

Revell launches the distinguished Grumman F-14A in 1981 as a highly detailed plastic model kit with all the bells and whistles on the large 1:32 scale.

The year 1981 was a year of transition. Revell USA and Revell UK still dominated the product planning, but the Bünde branch managed to develop the first products that we had asked for. Thus, Revell Germany received a BMW 318i in the American scale of 1:25, unfortunately in the version for the U.S. market with big fenders. A new truck series of the same size was just being launched in America. In addition, England requested a European truck. We at Bünde voted in this direction, too. For the German market, the developers decided to produce a Mercedes 1628 S, the imagery for which I did myself in the Wörth facility. Revell Great Britain relied on a Volvo Globetrotter. These two trucks and the American Peterbilt and Kenworth turned into best sellers, with countless varieties and evolutions produced over the years. However, other top sellers made their debut this year: for instance, the new 1:32-scale Tomcat, based on Tamiya quality, and a large 1:48-scale Sikorsky CH-53 G helicopter. Other than these, the program lived from the many snap models, an entire series of third-party products and editions, as well as tools that were also bought in from outside. Believe it or not, no less than 17 pages at the rear of the catalog were dedicated to accessories. Italeri articles were no longer included. Esci was still in the game, but with a separate catalog. One of the new items that we suggested, the BMW M1 in the wide Procar version, was also launched on the Dutch market in the "Jan Lammers" livery. A year later on the occasion of a Procar race in Zandvoort, Jan Lammers was presented the model officially. However, the Esci collection was deviating more and more towards military models, which certainly didn't dovetail with the product policies at Bünde. The signs were already pointing to an immenent end to the partnership. In this year, Taubert traveled to the Far East with Revell America's chief developer Ron Campbell. During this two-week trip, Campbell shared some very valuable tips about the job, about toolmaking, and, above all, about Revell's history in the USA. Many of these background stories were new to Taubert and are still largely unknown to the public today.

With the 1:24-scale Mercedes-Benz 1628 S, Revell breaks into the European truck scene and expands it the following year.

1982

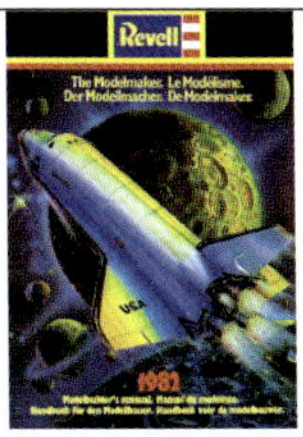

The Audi quattro makes its debut in 1:24-scale as a rally racer and the Volkswagen T3 Westfalia Joker with its 1:25-scale camper van interior proves to be another trump card.

The year 1982 heralded the beginning of the "bleak" times for us at Bünde, with a new marketing manager turning everything that had previously existed upside down. We deliberately withhold the name. Revell's image was given a makeover by a Frankfurt Agency, and not one stone was left unturned. The new slogan was clearly visible on the redesigned catalog title: Revell, The Modelmaker. The range was still dominated by typical American themes. But in 1982, too, Bünde managed to develop a few products that were crucial for the domestic markets. These included the hugely popular Buchmann-Porsche 928 as well as the VW Kombi T3 dubbed the "Westfalia Joker 2". For this I had very close ties to Westfalia in Wiedenbrück, who gave us incredible support with this project. Just to "think about" this project, the company even lent me an original motorhome to try out for a week. Although the end of the cooperation with Esci was a foregone conclusion, I still researched the brand-new original Audi quattro for my Italian colleagues. With this vehicle, Audi was taking a big step into a completely new brand and model policy. The Ur-quattro was the first all-wheel-drive sports car, which notched up sensational victories in rallying. After I'd gotten hold of an original vehicle from Audi via a circuitous route, the Ingolstadt manufacturer allowed us to hold on to it for one week so that we could undertake our research. I liked the car so much that I decided to buy it. After the BMW R 75/5 in 1971, this was my second vehicle that I'd been inspired by through my job. It wasn't easy to obtain, however, because at this time there were only a few demonstration vehicles in Germany at selected dealers, predominantly Porsche dealerships. According to the statement of the dealer I purchased the car from, Wehmeyer & Castrup in Bielefeld, I owned the first privately registered quattro in Germany. Several years of driving pleasure followed. The model, however, was dropped from the Revell range. The Jan Lammers version of the BMW M1 Procar, which had been developed the previous year, was presented to Jantje Lammers by Revell at a Procar race in Zandvoort this year. He, however, was so enthusiastic about my new Ur-quattro that he wanted to swap our cars before the race so that we could turn some laps at Zandvoort. The race director wasn't at all thrilled about this. What a pity!

During this year we also gained more experience on the topic of radio control, because Revell also took care of sales of this product for the Dutch company Veroma. The range of accessories also underwent a major rebranding, with terms such as "Contacta" for glue and Revell Color for the paints. But many images were still anything but attractive. The program was more balanced than ever, but still heavily influenced by America.

1983

With the giant Shell oil platform in the unconventional scale of 1:200 and the 1:87 tank engine from the 01 series, Revell searches for the right direction in 1983 for its model range.

This model year proved groundbreaking, because this year marked the start of what would be a long-standing and successful partnership with Jan Nannestad, the owner of the Danish company Heljan, as producer and mold-maker. Heljan, which was founded in 1957 in Odense, had already made a name for itself as the manufacturer of H0 railway accessories, but was also able to design tools for models alongside to the little railroad houses they built. Revell had fielded an interesting request from Shell Oil in England, with the invitation to manufacture an oil rig as a kit. No sooner said than done. Unusually, the research was not done on an original rig, instead, the dimensions and images would come from a large model, with technical sketches provided. At this stage, the Danish company was already involved in CAD construction techniques (computer-aided design), hence Revell could create its oil rig using this technology. The upshot of all this was that a model was built with a record-setting 36 individual tools. To this day, this exceptional product is regularly reissued. Our American colleagues also knocked on Heljan's door for assistance with the American car transporter in a scale of 1:25. Revell, however, had more exciting novelties up its sleeve for 1983. From the well-known *Jane's Report*, we reconstructed the concept of an F-19 Stealth Fighter in a 1:32 scale. This project would actually catch the eye of the CIA in the USA, who contacted us to ask where and how Revell obtained the information about this plane. Because *Jane's Report* is available to the public, the Revell managers didn't get thrown into jail. For the U.S. collection this year, Revell designed the most expensive tools in company history, the Rockwell B-1 Bomber in a scale 1:48. For Italeri, which had now suddenly been rediscovered as a partner, Taubert developed the 1:24 DAF 3300 truck, which was then incorporated into the product range. Revell had already flirted with the completely new idea of H0 locomotives during the Esci era, which we now developed for our own range. On a recommendation from Italeri, the entire project was implemented by an Italian toolmaker in Padua. This, too, was a step we never regretted in all the years to come. Thanks to the work with Heljan, Revell Germany was now in a position to develop its own smaller tools for additional parts for conversions of cars and trucks. All of this happened in 1983, as did the first series with History Makers: antique kits which arrived at customers in special packaging. Revell goes vintage.

1984

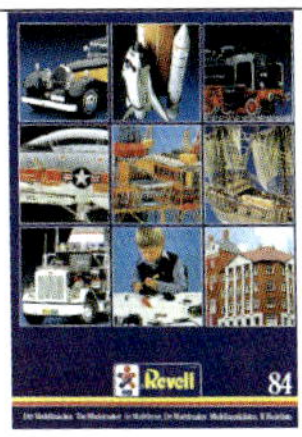

The coal excavator from O&K is the second industry giant that Revell miniaturizes with great success as a 1:200 plastic kit.

The year 1984 heralded the start of a new era and this was reflected in the new catalog title. The Ceji-Revell logo was simply obvious. The years under French direction were undoubtedly the most unpleasant in Revell history. This was because the French tried to eliminate Revell as a brand. Revell could have literally disappeared from the scene. Thanks to opposition from Revell's former managing director Kurt Haubrok, this didn't happen, however, as a compromise, the new owners were permitted to disfigure the logo. And they grabbed the opportunity. Once again, the models of this year benefited from an intense partnership with Heljan in Denmark. Probably the most outstanding product of this year was the Coal Excavator in a 1:200 scale. Again, it was impossible to photograph and measure an original, so for this job we took a large-scale model from the manufacturer Orenstein & Koppel in Lübeck and implemented this. The Excavator 289 is still occasionally reintroduced to the market and, like the Shell Oil Rig, is a hot item amongst collectors. The collaboration with Heljan in the H0 model range experienced such a phenomenal start that Revell decided to start manufacturing it themselves. The simply recipe for the development department was virtually 'on the doorstep'. While the collections of established H0 kit manufacturers were bursting exclusively with buildings typical of Bavaria and the Black Forest, Revell wanted to strike out in the direction of the "lowlands". Thus, a small series of farmhouses and some examples from the Bünde region resulted. Highly sought-after amongst enthusiasts today are the *Bünder Zollamt* (Customs House), Westfälische Bauernhof (Westphalian Farm), the *Bünder Tabakmuseum* (Tobacco Museum) and the *Posten 95* guardhouse. Heljan also delivered wagons for our existing steam locomotives. And we continued with aircraft such as the Airbus A310 and space projects like the Space Operation Center in Denmark.

But in 1984, Revell again shines a light into the vastness of space and has Denmark tailormake a so-called Laser Battle Station.

1985

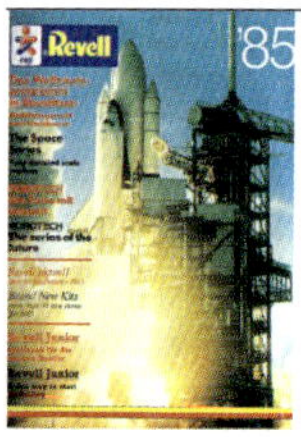

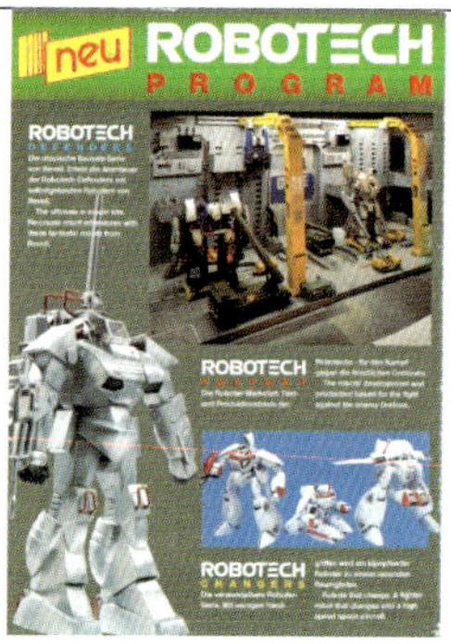

1985 is still dominated by the owner Ceji, who impose unmarketable products on Revell such as the Robotech. This is predestined to be nothing more than a huge flop.

This model year, too, fell under the auspices of Ceji in France. The collaboration with Heljan in Denmark, however, also gained momentum. Another large project stood in the wings, the Space Shuttle Launch Tower in 1:144, as a match to the Revell Space Shuttle. The original couldn't be accessed, of course, instead a large model provided the many images and drawings needed to create the model. From all of these documents, a model kit was created using CAD, and this kit is still reissued every now and then. In keeping with this and influenced by the success of the European space industry, we also developed the European Rocket Ariane 4 in Denmark, which didn't enjoy as much success on the retail market. Another spectacular new development was the Tornado, which had been in service in the German Air Force since 1982. Revell was eager to introduce it on the market in a scale of 1:32. The Revell team received first-class support in this from the troops, mainly from the naval aviation MFG 1 division in Schleswig-Jagel. At the base, Revell could use all the dimensions and take all the necessary photos. Jagel was chosen because the CAD designer from Heljan involved in the project had a relatively short journey to get there. Heljan also created additional parts for conversions. One project, however, was very clearly our PR highlight of the year: Based on the 1:32-scale Bo-105 from Italeri, we produced the Bo of the two-time world champion and world vice-champion in helicopter aerobatics, Captain Charly Zimmermann. The official model presentation was held on the occasion of Corpus Christi, June 6, 1985, at an airshow at the sports field in Bünde-Ahle, at which Charly demonstrated his world championship-winning freestyle skills with his Bo-105. The special model kit was a top seller in the Revell range for some years.

The "cooperation" with the French parent company Ceji brought forth such strange fruit that Ceji one day purchased containers full of robot kits from Japan and had them sent unannounced to Bünde. It was a financial and logistical problem that our former managing director Kurt Haubrok solved brilliantly.

With the 1:32-scale BO-105 in aerobatics uniform, Revell further expand an area that becomes one of the most successful: The range of detailed kits modeled on helicopters.

In a scale of 1:144, Revell returns to space. The Ariane 4 including a launch tower is new to the market, with the addition of a very detailed launch tower for the Space Shuttle as a plastic kit.

Revell also sets an example in 1985 with aircraft in the established 1:32 scale: The Panavia Tornado GR MK 1 from the Air Force is certainly a very interesting novelty for fans of airplane kits.

1986

The 1:24 Unimog from Revell now lines up to start the Paris-Dakar Rally and turns into an unexpected retail winner for the East Westphalians.

For Revell, the strategy to cut the French connection slowly became clear. Although Ceji was still the owner, Bünde reverted back to the old Revell logo. The front section of the catalog pointed mischievously to "30 Years of Revell". The program itself now also included items from various partnerships, for instance from the companies Lindberg, Fujimi, Tamiya and Heller. However, the German team also managed to launch several spectacular in-house developments. For example, the "industrial contract" with the Dutch shipping company Volker Stevin yielded the dredging vessel Geopotes 14 in the scale of 1:300. In conjunction with the automobile accessory manufacturer Kamei from Wiesbaden, Revell created the X1 car series: model cars that also received downsized Kamei add-on parts, as well as the corresponding rims and tires. The top product of 1986 was, however, the winning car of the Paris-Dakar Rally: the Mercedes Unimog of the Capito family in a scale of 1:24. Using this project as a baseline, Revell then became a sponsor of the Capito vehicle in 1986. This kit still enjoys cult status, and the basic model of the Unimog was then used as the basis for other body variants, including the TLF 8/18 fire truck. This fire-fighting truck would mark the start of a new series of fire engines in 1:24. The second model of this line in 1986 was a Ziegler LF 16 on a Mercedes-Benz 1017 chassis. Thanks to the intricate detailing, this and other fire engines joined the ranks of national and international top sellers. The originals used for the measurements and photos were found in the nearby Ruhr region and were readily available. All fire brigade units have supported our work without fail, and the same applies to the original manufacturer from whom Revell received the required material – unfailingly and always without a problem.

The paintwork on the intricate 1:32-scale model of the BO 105 PAH Hornisse makes it popular and underlines the increasing importance of special liveries in the aircraft sector.

Revell again sets sail on a big journey: The Gorch Fock is a recurring theme in the Revell program and the legendary tall ship again rounds out the broad spectrum of Revell products.

1987

Almost better than the Paris-Dakar version: the 1:24-Unimog of Revell as a winter-service variant with a large snowplow.

Again this year, Heljan was in high demand when it came to new developments. At the top of the list were the products Dornier 228 in a scale of 1:72, the 1:300 frigate F-122 Bremen, the 1:300 research vessel Meteor and, last but not least, the BK-117 in 1:32, a brand-new helicopter from a joint venture of MBB and Kawasaki. MBB provided exemplary backing for the project. Not only did they supply Revell with data and drawings, they also made the original demo helicopter available in a spectacular space-ship livery. From this year, this basis chopper turned into a top seller and was later sold in various versions. The catalog title very clearly shows where Revell's emphasis would lie in the truck sector: fire brigades. A new model was released in 1987: a Metz turntable ladder DLK 23-12 on a Mercedes-Benz 1422 chassis. Revell maintained ties to Metz in Karlsruhe for many years. As already mentioned, Revell sponsored the Capito team with their Unimog at this year's Paris-Dakar Rally. Unfortunately, this was the year that the rally organizer, Thierry Sabine, had a fatal accident during the race, which prompted the Capito team to pull out while in the lead – with its sponsor's agreement. The Unimog U 1300 was launched on the market immediately after the fire-fighting version, also as a municipal "winter-service" vehicle and in the Federal Armed Forces 2t Military version. These versions ensured that the Unimog would remain one of the best investments in toolmaking.

Revell's sleek Concorde plastic kit in a 1:144 scale and the MBB BK 117 as a 1:32-helicopter with a space-ship design make their debut.

1988

The Simba 8x8 in 1:24 is one of Revell's most important flagship projects in the commercial vehicle sector.

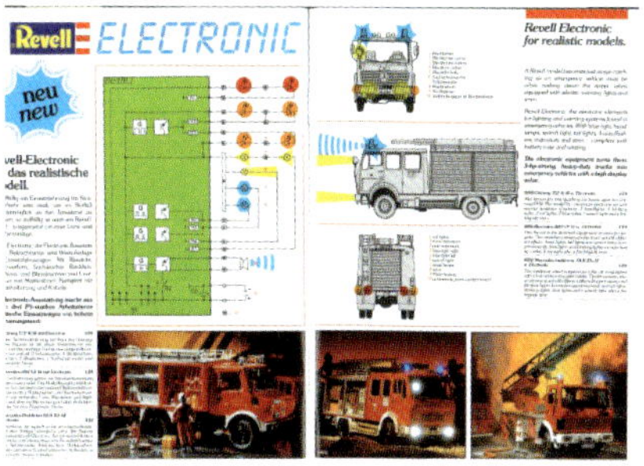

Electronics, too, in a 1:24-scale are part of the program and lend the fire departments sound and authentic-looking lights.

As revealed by the title of this year, Revell again wants to make a splash with an exceptionally spectacular model project: the GFLF Simba. For this project, there was exceptional teamwork with the Frankfurt Airport fire brigade. What emerged was the largest ever fire engine model kit, which enjoys huge popularity today, even with the many ongoing reissues. Another spectacular novelty was the 1:144-scale miniature of the F-19 Stealth Fighter, which had been previously scaled down to 1:48 and, in the 1:32-basis model from 1983, had caused all the previously mentioned problems with the CIA. It's still incomprehensible why this aircraft, which never actually existed in the original, turned into such a huge success. During this year, a partnership began that still exists today: the collaboration with the German Society for the Rescue of Shipwrecked Persons (DGzRS), or simply Sea Rescue. Based on the ship in service at that time, Revell made the model Berlin in a scale of 1:72. From the outset, working with team at its headquarters in Bremen proved exceptional, almost euphoric, with managing director Dr. Bernd Anders and press officer Andreas Lubkowitz pulling out all stops to help us promote the project on their behalf. From photo appointments on board, media trips, model presentations right through to events for the press on board, we received incredible support. At the same time, Revell became one of the patrons of the Sea Rescue Service, by way of donating a set sum to the DGzRS from each kit we sold. Today we have a license fee. Over time, a total of more than 150,000 Euro was received by the DGzRS. The proposal to name one of the upcoming boats "Bunde" is in the pipeline, we are now waiting to see if it will be implemented at some stage. Revell also launched another new product line called Premium, with 1:24-scale car model kits, which with over 200 individual parts were significantly more demanding and of higher quality than the standard line. Eventually, more developments would follow. Also released this year, the new Golf II with a 16-valve engine, a car I also made my own and in which I experienced more than 150,000 kilometers of huge enjoyment. During this year I also made a particularly interesting acquaintance: While developing the models Avalanche and Cyrrus I had the pleasure of meeting Uwe Gemballa, the well-known Porsche customizer. He was an extremely amiable man, okay he wore a Rolex, but he was down-to-earth and he loved model kits. This encounter was one of the most special during my time at Revell.

1989

Revell dedicates a 1:24 model to the ultimate cult roadster, the BMW Z1, which even features cool, retractable doors.

This year would be characterized by several trendsetting model developments. The catalog title already highlighted a new Electronics series with various types of models. This line was way ahead of its time and would remain in the catalog for years. Similar to the previous Eurofighter, the new PAH.2 helicopter in a 1:48 scale is created following a 1:1 mock-up model made of wood. The real combat helicopter from the German army would be implemented much later, of course with many changes that the mock-up model would eventually receive. Revell finally pushed a large 1:32-scale Dornier Do 27 out of the hangar that had long been in the planning. Here, too, the incredible help I received from the eventual Revell managing director Hans-Ulrich Remfert at a photo shoot in Pfaffenhofen was a unique and unforgettable experience. An extremely interesting model development was the Baltic Sea ferry T.S. Finnjet. On the initiative of the operator, the Silja Line in Finland, we worked closely with them to implement this large ferry. This proved a sensation at this time because the model ships were very much military-focused. The 1:400 kit proved exceptionally popular with the public. A little side story about this: We arranged with the shipping company to hold our four-day annual sales conference, which also included the presentation of new articles, on board the Finnjet. The cost for the entire seminar was covered by “trading”, in other words, with a kit quota for the Silja Line. Just to mention in passing, after our stay in Helsinki, our rolling warehouse, the Revell campervan, was forgotten in the harbor. Another major step in the development of Revell models was the purchase of the complete 1:24 die-cast collection from the Esci company. For us ,the investment in another big mainstay was because the company Bburago was enjoying huge success in the 1:24 and 1:18 models. These tools were used in the form of both assembled models and metal kits. This year marked a huge step forward for Germany with the Berlin wall coming down on November 9. Unfortunately the catalog had already been printed by this stage, otherwise we would have made mention of this momentous occasion. In terms of future product development, however, the opening of the Hungarian-Austrian border on 11 September gave the green light for new ideas.

The imposing Finnjet ferry in a 1:400 scale was a Revell sensation; the SL Roadster in 1:24 is a star in the car range in the year 1989.

Revell picks up the pace in the aircraft segment in 1989. The 1:72 Eurocopter UHT/HAP makes its debut, with Revell bringing a modern classic on the market with the 1:32 Dornier Do 27.

1990

Revell likes the 850i. Not only is the coupé released in Bünde as a 1:24-plastic kit, but also as die-cast models in the scales of 1:18 and 1:24.

The brand new BMW 850i, which we'd integrated into our Premium line, graced the catalog title of this year. At this time, we were lucky enough to have an extremely approachable contact at BMW. Gerhard Gutjahr would end up working alongside us for years and every project with him was great fun. In the car sector we then unveiled one of the most well-known Revell car models at the trade fair. This vehicle, the Trabant in a 1:24 scale, symbolized the fall of the Berlin Wall. In September of the previous year, I was on my way back from the Danish toolmaker, when I suddenly came across a convoy of these two-stroke cars coming opposite me on the autobahn. The border was open and thousands of GDR citizens grabbed their chance to visit the "West". I hadn't even made it back to the office when I got the order from management to develop a 1:24 "Trabi". The catch, however, was that it had to be ready in time for the 1990 trade fair. No problem. In the unprecedented record time of no less than four months, our team had developed a kit. Admittedly, it was in a simplified version, with many compromises and relatively few individual parts, but it had great detailing and was perfect as a finished model. The model was delivered to the 1990 trade fair and afterwards became the best-selling car model in history of Revell's model-making. The "Trabi" wasn't the only highlight of that year. We reintroduced an earlier idea from America with car kits in the scale of 1:16 and brought the classic split-screen "Pretzel" Beetle on the market. Although it was publicized as a 1952 model, the original was a mix of the 1952 and 1953 Beetles, which led to a heated discussion amongst modeler's. After great success with the Finnjet, we decided to add another civilian vessel to our shipping fleet. In this, too, we wanted to strike out on new paths and we opted for a Rhine passenger ship, the museum paddle steamer Goethe. At this time we were selling 80 percent of our products on the German market, and thus the Goethe also became a top seller for several years. I

Premium stands for a new Revell kit series. Shown here is the BMW 750 iL in 1:24.

still clearly remember the official press event with the model presentation with the Köln-Düsseldorfer river cruise operator on board the Rhine steamship. On this occasion, too, our eventual managing director Hans-Ulrich Remfert was assigned the job as head of marketing. For the first time, the die-cast models got their own catalog. The contents, of course, came from the former 1:24-scale die-cast line of Esci, and also the first 1:18-models, which were still being finished with Revell USA playing the leading role. Thus, the Ford Thunderbird was created for the U.S. market and the Mercedes-Benz 500 SL (R129) for the German market. And for the smaller 1:24-scale kits, new cars were created initially, such as the BMW Z1, 850i, and the Gemballa Avalanche – all based on already existing plastic kits.

The paddle steamer Goethe of the Köln-Düsseldorfer line impresses here as an assembled model in the scale 1:160 and as a fitting illustration for the box of this large ship model miniature.

1991

With the BMW 507 Roadster in 1:18 as a finished die-cast model and in 1:24 as a plastic kit, Revell launches two different models of the iconic roadsters from the blue-and-white marque.

The catalog title pointed out that this year would be characterized by a sensational promotion. The design of race trucks in 1:24 was tied to a commitment as the main sponsor of the Truck Grand Prix at the Nürburgring. Revell initially made models of the frontrunners in the European Truck Championship, both Mercedes-Benz – more would follow. The newly introduced articles this year were also connected to some unforgettable personal contacts. For instance, the Boeing 767 in the colors of Lauda Air. It just so happened that I was in Seoul for a model authorization and I met Niki Lauda in my hotel who autographed the box of the new model for me. We also had the first novelty in the 1:72-scale aircraft line, which had been created by Axel Dietz, the former head designer of Plasticart in the GDR. Axel Dietz had previously made the assembly instructions and box illustrations for us. A special experience was a meeting with Sergio Pininfarina, whose design concept Mythos based on the Testarossa had been launched on the market in both the 1:24-scale plastic kit and a 1:18-scale die-cast model. We also developed the BMW 507, arguably the most beautiful BMW ever, in plastic and metal. On top of the great cooperation with Gerhard Gutjahr from BMW, I also got to personally meet Albrecht Graf Goertz at his Brunkensen manor near Alfeld/Leine. As a designer, Count Goertz had created the 503 and 507 for the American BMW importer Loewy in the fifties – today, both cars have truly iconic designs. I had the pleasure of spending an entire day with this world famous designer.

Electronics add a lot of glitz. A perfect example is this Chevy Show Van from 1991 in the large 1:16-scale made in the USA.

With the Mercedes race truck in 1:24, Revell opens up a whole new avenue and visits the racetracks with PR stands. In contrast, the MIG-29B in 1:32 seems almost conventional. With the planned MBB concept Sänger, Revell once again go stratospheric and orchestrates yet another breathtaking concept.

1992

None other than the Pink Floyd drummer Nick Mason lends Revell his Ferrari 250 GTO for the model research. The 1:12 model still fetches top prices amongst enthusiasts and in 1992 represented a milestone in the market for die-cast miniatures.

After Revell had split up the various model categories within its product development, I could focus more and more on my favorite area of cars, motorbikes and trucks. Although I would also occasionally come up with a different model types. In 1992, the truck racing theme was expanded, this time with the winning vehicle of 1991, the Pheonix MAN driven by Gerd Körber. We again hosted a huge PR event during the Truck Grand Prix at the Nürburgring, combined with a party that I've never forgotten. Revell then released the most valuable car in the Mercedes Museum as a model: the Mercedes 300 SLR world famous Uhlenhaut-Coupe. This was made possible thanks to our former contact person at Mercedes-Benz Classic and my future friend, Friedrich Müller. With him, we turned a whole series of Daimler types into models. Working with him and receiving his support was always terrific. In the headlines of this year was the rebirth of the Bugatti marque. Revell had decided to produce the new Bugatti EB 110 as a model and I had the job of contacting the former owner Romano Artioli in Campogalliano near Modena. For me, it was amazing that the big boss took a personal interest in this model. There was an even bigger story behind the styling concept of Giorgio Giugiaro's Italdesign, the Nazca M12 based on the BMW 850 which was first unveiled in Tokyo in 1991. We had decided that this super sports car should also be released as a 1:24-scale model and a 1:18 die-cast model. The M12 was the first concept car from Fabrizio Giugiaro, with whom I had close contact over the years. A licensing agreement was mandatory, but it came with no financial obligations. The die-cast model was planned to come out before the plastic kit and we had just produced 20,000 of this model in China. We received an interim injunction from the BMW legal department, forbidding us to use the BMW kidney grille on our model. Giugiaro had been granted an exception for the original, but not for the model, which I couldn't comprehend at all, because the concept had been built specifically for BMW. Hence, we had to remove all the kidneys from the models – thank heavens they were all separate plastic parts – and replace them with a simple oval. I asked for the plastic grilles that were no longer required and several days later I sent those 20,000 small kidneys by registered post to the BMW legal department for their further use. Of course I didn't get a response. Without the BMW kidney, the model, of course, became less interesting for collectors because it no longer corresponded to the original. Another spectacular product was the Ferrari 250 GTO as a large 1:12-scale die-cast model. With only 36 originals built, I had the problem of tracking one down in order to take photos and measurements. It took weeks for the Ten Tenth Collection in England to agree put a GTO at our disposal. Behind this collection of racing sports car was the drummer of Pink Floyd, Nick Mason. I then met up with Nick at the Oldtimer Grand

Although the Nazca concept of Fabrizio Giugiaro features the BMW kidney grille, Revell had to remove these on both 1:24 and 1:18-scale models and thus drastically change the nose of the miniature shortly before the start of production.

für die Ital-
Fabrizio Giugiaro's
Interesse am
– besonders
und Gruppe C –
diesem Entwurf

und die Basis für
Teamwork mit allen
Beteiligten.
Das Ergebnis ist ein Traum
zum Anfassen: Der neue
Nazca M 12.

7345 Italdesign Nazca M 12 1:24

Eine Giugiaro-Auto-Vision

Dies ist ein Gran Turismo von jenem Stoff, aus dem die Zukunfts-Träume der Autofahrer von heute gedacht, gezeichnet und gemacht werden.

Höchstwertige technische Bausteine in möglichst einfacher Montagetechnik, verpackt in einem Maßanzug, der durch seine zwingende Formgebung besticht.

Ein als Mittelmotor längs eingebauter BMW-12-Zylinder mit 300 PS treibt die Hinterräder an, getragen von einem Carbon-Fiber-Chassis mit Rohrrahmen und Kunststoff-Karosse.

Der konsequente Zweisitzer zeigt ein ganz typisches Giugiaro-Merkmal: Die Türen sind horizontal zweigeteilt. Die untere Hälfte ist eine normale Autotür, die obere verglaste Hälfte reicht jeweils bis mitten ins Dach hinein und öffnet sich nach oben wie beim legendären Mercedes 300 SL Gullwing.

Bestechend an der flachen Karosserie ist die Möglichkeit, Seitenfenster und hintere Dachschale ganz auszuhängen, um in Sekunden ein Cab... durch Sonne und Wind zu ...

Im Maßstab 1:24 ein... Auto-Vision von ... Modellqualität ... Auto-...

In 1992, Revell miniaturized a milestone in civilian aviation with the 1:72-scale model of the Junkers F-13.

Prix at the Nürburgring and we talked through the whole project, which he then supported brilliantly. I still have a hand-signed GTO with the wooden plaque from our first series.

1993

At the Tokyo Motor Show, the Audi Avus quattro celebrates its debut. Revell produces thc super sports car with four rings from Ingolstadt as a finished die-cast zinc model in a scale of 1:18 with a chrome body. Later it would be made in plastic as a 1:43 finished model.

In the car sector, the perfect partnership with Friedrich Müller from Daimler-Benz continued. For this year we developed the Mercedes 300 SLR in the Mille Miglia winning version driven by Stirling Moss. With the Bugatti EB 110, which had been produced the previous year, Revell launched a new series with 1:43-scale preassembled models, which only actually existed for a couple of years. Since zinc die-cast models were experiencing a boom, we decided to go down this track as well and added a new 1:24 truck series as well as a 1:12 motorbike line. Parallel to launching the then-new generation of flat engines and the BMW R 1100 RS, Revell had also begun with world-famous vintage motorbike, in our case with the MV Agusta 750s. For the trade fair showcasing new products, at which the MV debuted, I was lucky enough to present a rare original and the most successful motorbike rider of all time: the 15-time world champion, Giacomo Agostini. Meeting this motorbike legend was a very special experience for me, because during my active days as a motorcyclist I'd practically followed Agostini at his European rounds of the world championship. Revell expanded its 1:12 die-cast line with the 300 SLR Uhlenhaut-Coupe, here as well with the exceptional backing of Friedrich Müller from Mercedes Classic Center. He even made it possible for us to show the original million-dollar museum gem at our new product show. A very important milestone in my time as development head was the Audi Avus project. This design concept, which was unveiled to the public at the 1991 Tokyo Motor Show, was crying out to be made into a 1:18 model. At that time, Thomas Frank had just started his job at Audi as the head of PR and was promptly entrusted with the model-car topic. Thus, our Avus was the first model project to receive official support and guidance from Audi. I recall collecting the first model off the assembly line and taking it to Ingolstadt to present to Thomas Frank. While we were talking, the head of development Franz-Josef Paefgen intervened and wanted to confiscate the first autographed sample model, however a model of this series still holds pride of place on Thomas Frank's desk. Revell still has exemplary and close ties to Audi. Thanks to a solid personnel policy at Audi, we are able to continue working with former Audi staff such as Thomas Frank and Marc Hufenbecher. After the BMW Isetta, the Avus turned into our second best-selling die-cast model.

The Alexander von Humboldt with its green sails makes a striking impression. It provides a magnificent model for a detailed plastic kit in a 1:150-scale. Moreover, a beer brand made the royal tall ship even more famous thanks to many advertising spots on TV.

1994

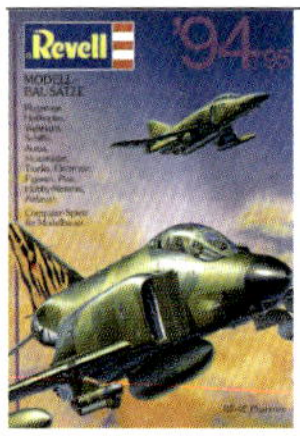

Revell experts develop the beautifully designed, first-generation Volkswagen Karmann Ghia as a large plastic 1:16-scale model and give it moving doors and hoods. T charming two-door car from Osnabrück immediately dri its way into the hearts of model-car makers.

Revell once again came up with a raft of ideas for this year, beginning with the Kids & Kits club through to new model lines such as CD-ROM and Mini-Dinos. We welcomed the merger with Monogram by launching a separate Monogram Europe line. For the finished models, we forged a tie with Gonio, a manufacturer of tin models. This year marked a special anniversary, 25 years since the moon landing. A whole series of old molds were reissued for this occasion. A new cooperation began with Protar from Italy and this would endure over many years. I had the pleasure of meeting Tarquinio Provini, the two-time motorbike world champion and founder of Protar. Out of his passion for motorbikes he founded the company that produced motorbike kits in a 1:9 scale. His son, Marzio, and I are still close friends. Our first project together was a Harley Davidson. Protar didn't have a European license for its products, but instead delivered exclusively to one U.S. customers. We then began bit by bit to market Protar's collection under Revell. The Porsche Boxster was to be another spectacular novelty in the die-cast segment. In very close liaison with the design team at Weissach, over months I developed the 1:18 and the new 1:43 model and implemented all the changes made along the way. When we finally got the approval for the original model of the Boxster after a great deal of toing and froing, our competition had already brought out the finished model. The project was stopped immediately and, of course, never realized. The resulting damage was neither quantified nor discussed, because unfortunately the approval procedure is always up to the licensor and in this case it went against us. For years after this "incident", Revell avoided taking on any more Porsche models. There was, however, another 1:18 die-cast product that would be launched this year: the BMW Isetta. Since the beginning of our die-cast activities in 1990 I had repeatedly insisted on developing cars from the

Even the box illustration of the Tyrannosaurus Rex is enough to give goose bumps. Luckily the model isn't bigger than 1:13.

fifties (the time of the economic miracle), this time I finally got the green light for this project. Prior to this one of our three board members would always ask: "Who would buy such a product?" This year I received the go-ahead from two other board members, Kurt Haubrok and Uli Remfert. They weren't disappointed. The Isetta would ultimately become the most successful Revell model ever and, with sales of more than a million units, is only beaten by the Ferrari F40 from Bburago. This record still stands today. A valuable partner and supporter of this idea was Gerhard Gutjahr from BMW, whose announcement that BMW wanted to order quite a large fleet for themselves contributed significantly to this positive outcome.

Revell sells over a million units of the BMW Isetta in 1:18, making it the best-selling model in this scale. Revell even produce a separate catalog for the zinc die-cast models in the scales of 1:12, 1:18, 1:20, 1:24 and 1:43. The Porsche Boxster as a 1:18 model is also announced in the catalog, however it unfortunately never appears on the market.

1995

Revell never runs out of fantasty. In 1995, the German firm launches a new model on the market: the airship Hindenburg in the unconventional scale of 1:720. This breathtaking kit is even delivered to customers with a matching anchoring tower.

The title of the 1995 catalog very clearly highlighted that we put the main focus on motorbikes and the Harley Davidson brand. Over six pages, Revell presented 22 models in the scales of 1:8, 1:9 and 1:12. With the helicopters, the outdated Bo-105 was followed by its successor: the Eurocopter EC-135 prototype. In this case, too, we created a model out of the first demo chopper, which would eventually receive a few modifications and go into production. Nevertheless, with this model, Revell beat the original to the market by a year. In the ship line, we once again rifled through Jane's Report and found a stealth boat called the Sea Shadow. Using only one photo, the design department conjured up a model – this time, however, without a visit from the CIA. Ferrari celebrated its 50th anniversary and for the occasion planned a successor to the F40. For the purpose of confidentiality, the new F50 was shown neither as a Coupé nor as a Spider in our catalog – only covered with a tarp. The photo session took place in complete secrecy in Maranello. We weren't actually allowed to take the images ourselves, instead an in-house photographer had to do the job. A side note: Back then we researched the first F50 that rolled off the assembly line and this car – like all other Ferraris with the chassis number 1 – was painted yellow. This is actually the color ex-works; red is only available as an optional extra. Formula One would become an ongoing theme in our program and this year we focused on the Benetton-Ford of Michael Schumacher, with which he then became world champion for the first time. Many still vividly remember the children's airbrush system Painterman from this year, unfortunately it appeared on the market a year too early, and the product wasn't completely ready. The die-cast range grew with many different versions of the Isetta, each version an outstanding success. From Daimler and again with strong support from our friend Friedrich Müller, we developed the Mercedes 300 SE "fintail". This would be followed by more versions and anecdotes.

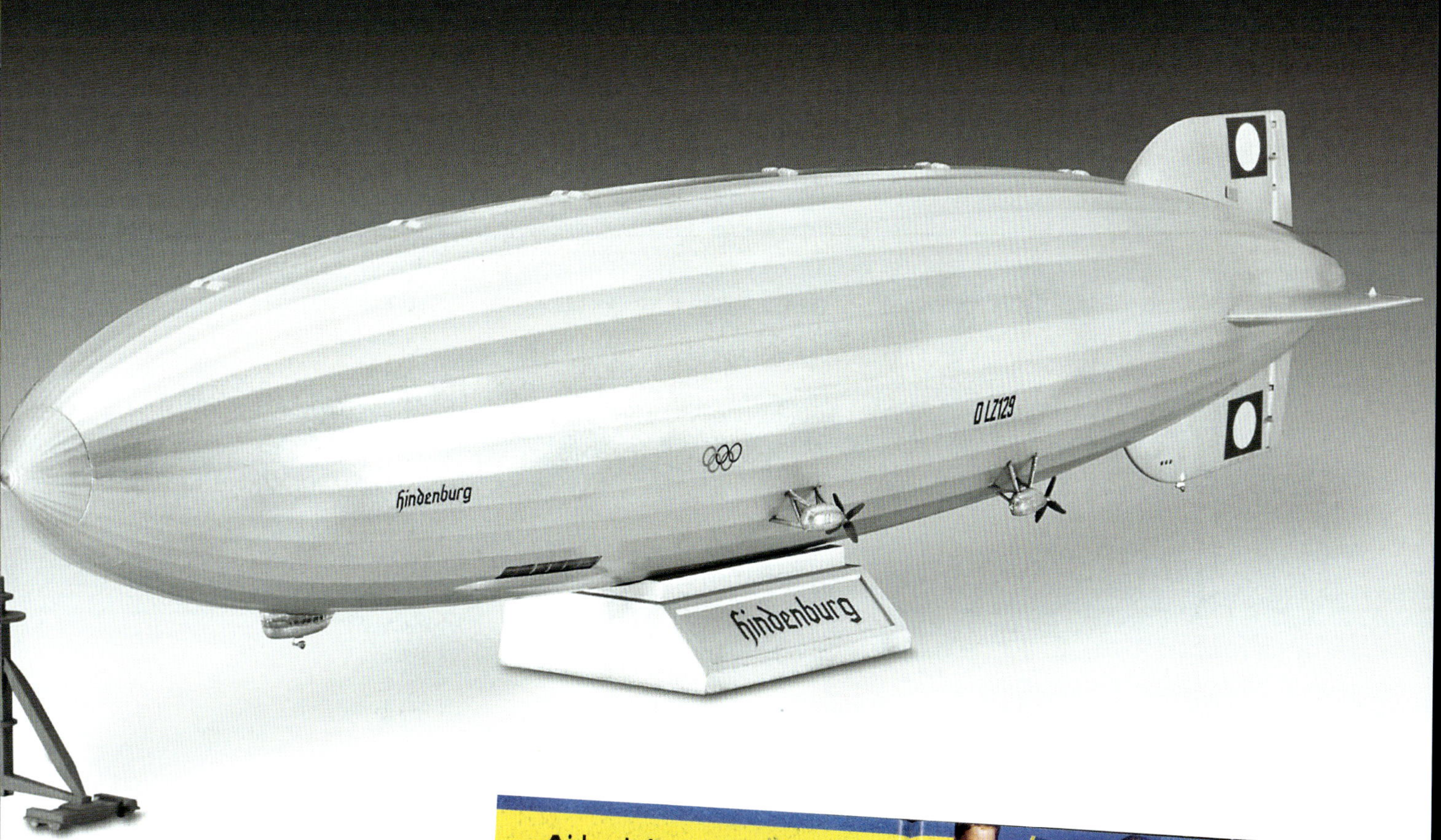

Sometimes manufacturers can be too far ahead of the times. Revell experiences this fate with its Painterman project, an airbrush kit for children to paint on paper and other templates. The technology, however, is simply not yet advanced enough and hence a good idea never really goes into production.

1996

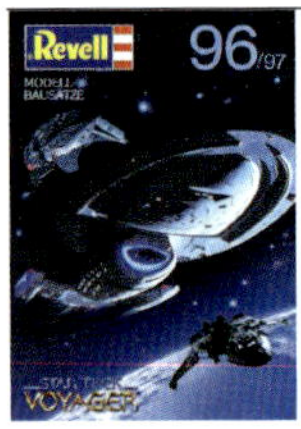

Some unkind critics liken the Messerschmitt Kabinenroller to "people in aspic". Revell simply ignore this and immortalize the bubble car from the economic miracle in a 1:18 model.

During this year I was once again responsible for a helicopter project that Revell had been planning to implement for years: The Alouette II. My close ties with the Army Aviation Corp at Bückeburg, where a friend of mine was a flight instructor, helped me with this project. He opened the door for Revell when it came to the original, photographing and measuring. I then had the 1:32 model made by the Danish toolmaker. The Formula One grid continued to grow, this time by adopting products from the Protar range and, of course, the Ferrari theme as well. In the military area I got the green light for the first model without a cannon, the 1:35 Unimog 1300 of the German army in 1:35, which Revell produced as a scale-down on the basis of our 1:24 models. The die-cast line also grew with the next "economic miracle car", the Messerschmitt Kabinenroller (Cabin Scooter). Following the Isetta concept, we also marketed the "Karo" in many different versions and color combinations. This model, too, sold very well and is still one of the most-produced die-cast products. With the BMW Isetta we started an experiment that was intended as a PR gag, but became very successful: the so-called "Football Isetta". Renowned Bundesliga Clubs, with the exception of Bayern München, took part in this. All 5,555 units of the Schalke 04 and Borussia Dortmund limited edition series sold out immediately. The project even went so far that some fans then acquired an original based on our models, for instance Arminia Bielefeld, Schalke 04 and Borussia Mönchengladbach, and had them painted like the Revell model.

In the military scale of 1:35, the Unimog celebrates its model kit debut as a two-ton Bundeswehr truck in Revell's program.

The Aerospatiale Alouette II boosts the fleet of Revell helicopters and, in the scale of 1:32, underlines how the delicate rotor blades can be shrunk in size as a plastic model. Note the interior layout of the cockpit and the reproduced subtleties in the turbine of the Bundeswehr chopper.

1997

Another real highlight at Revell would turn heads this year. An enquiry from the Transrapid Consortium in Kassel triggered discussions. As this new eco-friendly technology was to be sold, the manager needed a model for marketing. For the target group, however, not as a plastic kit, but as a ready-painted and decorated model, the parts of which only had to be clicked into place. A wonderful miniature suitable for the H0-gauge railway emerged, which at that time sold very well. Unfortunately, the consortium canned the whole project, but only after transferring the entire technology to China. The cooperation with Protar in 1997 yielded more kits of Ferrari Formula One cars, and also a new 1:9 motorbike range with the likes of Ducati, Cagiva and Kawasaki. Another sensation was the first truck in a 1:24 scale based on a model from the fifties: the legendary Büssing 8000. This beautiful model is still being reissued today and is always a favorite with hobbyists. Conceived by our in-house designer Klaus Lassen, the Büssing would mark the start of a complete series of trucks from the economic miracle era. In the military ranks, we discovered that due to the impending Kosovo war, the Bundeswehr took on a new role as a "peacekeeping troop". From one day to the next, the German army gained a positive image, which meant that nothing now stood in the way of developing the military vehicles or tanks that had been declined up until that point. First I developed the 1:35-scale Marder followed by the Fuchs armored vehicle, with tremendous support from a long-standing friend and military expert, Michael Jerchel. His contact to the Bundeswehr and the relevant agencies enabled us to take photos mainly in the Armored Troops School in Munster. It goes without saying that I continued with the next die-cast vintage model from the fifties. During this year we produced the Goggomobil T 250, and other versions of the Kabinenroller and Isetta were released.

At times Revell can also think big. The Büssing 8000 was launched in a 1:24 scale with vintage trucks, some of which had to be assembled with around 300 parts. The suspension and engine are portrayed here with great attention to detail. This model is recommended for ambitious modelers.

Revell once again dares to come up with new ideas in 1997. Proof of this is the Transrapid, which is launched on the market as a 1:87 scale model. The Bünde team expands its compact car series with the legendary Goggomobil in 1:18.

With the military vehicles in the 1:35 scale, Revell also continues to work on its own broad-based program, as demonstrated by the TPz1 Fuchs, which appears in specialist retail stores as a plastic kit.

1998

With the Dassault Rafale in 1:48, Revell relies on another modern fighter jet for its 1998 plastic kits, which the developers at Bünde meticulously recreate with a great deal of detailing and a complete jet cockpit.

This year for the first time, Revell went online, announced with a prominent separate section in the catalog. The title itself highlights that Formula One would be the core topic of the year thanks to “Schumi-mania”. After Benetton, Jordan and Williams, this year saw Ferrari and its arch rival McLaren joining the grid in a 1:24 scale. Racing in general continued to play a major role this year. The sensational truck series from the fifties was systematically continued with the addition of a 1:24 Krupp Titan. The military series received another 1:35 model with the SpPz Luchs. The die-cast sector expanded with the next economic miracle car, the Lloyd Alexander. This model, too, would eventually be sold in several colors and model versions, resulting in a steady growth in overall circulation. I would also develop another mass produced car, the fourth-generation Volkswagen Golf. With this project, developed parallel to the original, I was able to experience for the first time a “new kind of cooperation” with a manufacturer. During initial discussions about our project with VW, I had the dubious pleasure of meeting about a dozen participants of the Golf IV project. The implementation of the original into a model proved to be extremely difficult, because each of the people involved wanted to assert their influence and ultimate have the last word on the small model. The whole matter culminated in the fact that at the eleventh hour the handle for the trunk lid had to be changed on the original, because the then CEO didn’t like it. Due to time constraints VW resorted to using existing materials, in this case taking the hatchback handle from the Polo. We also had to do this at the very last minute, but that’s what the licensing agreement dictated. After this experience I stayed away from turning brand-new mass production cars into models. On the back of the catalog we alluded to a sensational new development from Audi, the Audi TT, which for reasons of secrecy was only shown as a silhouette under a tarp. This development would run completely differently and without any problems.

The legendary Krupp Titan writes history in the vintage truck scene with the 1:24-scale model. The SpPz Luchs expands the brand's range of 1:35-scale military vehicles.

1999

Revell, too, can't resist the fascination of the Borgward brand. The beautiful 1:18-scale Isabella rolls into the limelight as a finished die-cast model. Later, even prettier variations would follow in a stylish two-tone paint finish.

1999 would be a year of surprises and new personal acquaintances. As part of the general science fiction trend with *Babylon5* and *Star Trek*, Revell hit on the idea of making a model of the well-known German science fiction series *Perry Rhodan*. In very close contact with the publisher, Pabel Moewig Verlag in Rastatt, and the in-house illustrator Alfred Kelsner from Bünde, Revell developed science fiction models that had thrilled *Perry Rhodan* readers. A project earmarked specifically for children and teenagers were the models for the popular TV series *Käpt'n Blaubär* broadcast as part of WDR's *Sendung mit der Maus*. The difficulty with this project, in which the sailing ship and the five figures had to be realized, was that two-dimensional documents and scripts had to be turned into 3D models. The result was simple pre-painted snap kits, which were intended for beginners. Unfortunately, the project never really took off as expected. We wanted to take on a completely different license from the comic scene on the launch of a new movie. The model for the new Werner movie *Satte Literschüssel* (a motorbike) was to become one of my greatest adventures and experiences. My first meeting with the Wernersens (Rötger "Brösel" and Andi Feldmann) made me realize that the contents of the comic were not too far from reality. For a model we always needed an "oginool", but this wasn't to be the case with Werner. Instead, they supplied us with just the front fork of the bike with a wheel. "Easy, make a model out of that!" (quote from Brösel). The rest were sketches on serviettes, beer mats and other surfaces. The story of how *Satte Literschüssel* was created is enough to fill an entire book. After a year of development work, I had the pleasure of flying with the two to Bologna for the tool inspection and approval. This journey is indelibly etched in my memory: from the destroyed television set in the airport hotel at Hanover to the incredibly meticulous model presentation at Protar through to a very much delayed flight because the Werners wanted to buy bottles and bottles of olive oil "as souvenirs for friends". However, at the end of the day, the whole adventure with Brösel and Andi was huge fun, although it sometimes pushed the tolerance boundaries. We kept in touch for years. The die-cast sector veered away from the compact car range, but stayed true to the fifties and sixties era: this time with the Borgward Isabella as a coupé. When we realized that no one had name and property rights for

The first Audi TT is still regarded as an unrivaled style icon today. Revell launches the shapely coupé from Ingolstadt as a ready-made model in the Bburago-scale of 1:18 and thus enjoys unexpected sales success.

In 1999, Revell unveils no less than four models following the *Perry Rhodan* book project theme. One of them is the huge Marco Polo spaceship with its astonishing detailing. Sought-after by Sci-Fi fans.

The *Satte Literschüssel* by Werner in a scale of 1:9 gives Revell a huge boost. *Kapitän Blaubär*, on the other hand, spins yarns on his Revell sailing ship that would make even a sailor blush.

this, Revell applied and received the approval. The highlight of the 1:18 models was, however, the long-kept secret brand-new Audi TT, which we managed to develop parallel to the original. This time, however, with excellent support from Thomas Frank and Marc Hufenbecher from Audi AG. After the Isetta, Avus and Kabinenroller, the TT would become one of the most successful 1:18 projects of all time.

2000

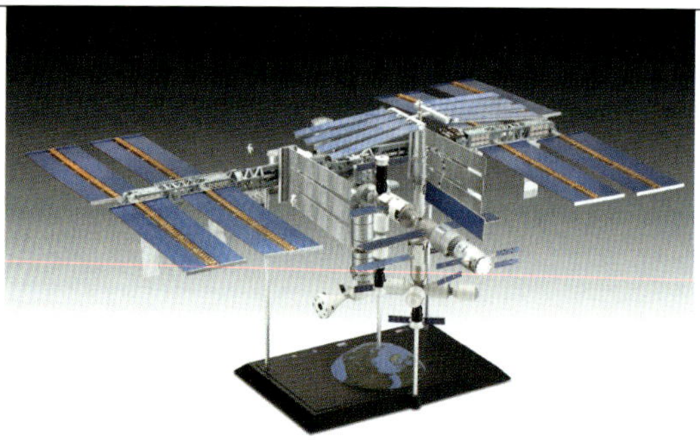

In a scale of 1:144, the Revell designers even venture into the realm of the International Space Station (ISS) at the turn of the millennium and include a tiny astronaut as a suitable size comparison.

With the turn of the millennium, I turned more and more of my attention to marketing matters in product development, and the projects were increasingly taken care of by project managers. I cut back on the number of models I developed myself to concentrate more on general matters such as exhibitions, club meetings, trade fairs and looking after interns. However, I also helped with selected new developments. One of these was the first CAD project, a benchmark project so to speak, the model of a Russian vehicle, the Ekranoplan. We had to implement this project with virtually no technical material, only with images and photos from publications. This then became our first in-house CAD project. We also took the sensational newcomer from BMW for our catalog title, the new BMW Z8, which also played an important role in a James Bond movie. A new Mini was also designed as a 1:24 model, but this was done by a project manager. Because of my contacts to Munster and Augustdorf trucks of the German army, I developed 10, 7 and 5-ton trucks, namely from the MAN family, as 1:35-scale models for our military range. The die-cast line, which I was still responsible for, took off with the Buckel-Volvo PV series and the NSU TT. This, too, resulted in top quality finished models thanks to excellent assistance from Volvo "guru" Paul Uckelmann from Coesfeld and Ralph Plagmann from Audi Tradition.

The BMW Z8 plays a major role in the James Bond spy movie *The World Is Not Enough*. Revell develops the white-and-blue retro roadster from Munich as a 1:24-model with an authentic-looking V8 under the hood.

These three products emphasis the sheer breadth of Revell's range in the year 2000: The legendary Buckel-Volvo PV series (top) is produced as a ready-made metal model in the 1:18 scale. The Zeppelin NT (bottom left) attracts attention as a 1:200-scale plastic kit, and the Ekranoplan A-90 Orljonok hovers over the water in 1:144.

2001

Revell and the four rings go well together. In 2001, a 1:18-scale die-cast model of the Auto Union Type C Streamline joins the range as a newcomer.

Once again I was lucky enough to receive help from my friends at the Army Aviation Corp in Bückeburg. Revell wanted to release the German army training version of the new EC-135 so we conducted the product research there.
In the car segment we expanded our horizons this year to include not only Formula One racers but a new series of road-going Ferrari sports cars. Revell's good and long-standing contact with Maranello put us in the position of having the exclusive right to create these models. Apart from Revell, only Tamiya in Japan received the occasional Ferrari license. I also developed a new series of aircraft for young modelers, and we called them Easy Kits. The main priority with these kits was that they should be colorful and simple to assemble. Revell had realized at this time that it was very important to look after our young customers so that there would be enough modelers in the future. This series has survived to this day and over the years has been successfully adopted by teenagers in hundreds of model-making activities. The die-cast sector boomed this year with six completely new developments, the highlight of which was Revell's New Mini in the super-scale 1:12. But one project was to be another very special experience: The Red Porsche Killer, arguably the most famous motorbike of the Werners. I could fill pages with the story of how this model came about. Thank goodness this time we got an original to use as the basis, which we easily reproduced into a 1:9 model. An anecdote on the side: We were forbidden by Porsche to call the model the same as the "Oginool", hence we used the name Red XXXXXXX Killer on both the packaging and the decals. On the occasion of the Revell show we invited the "Red Porsche Killer", the Satte Literschüssel and the two creators Rötger and Andi Feldmann to Bünde – an unforgettable experience.

In the large 1:12 scale, Revell takes on the new Mini and produces the tiny cult car as a die-cast miniature.

The diesel locomotive Ludmilla BR 230 (top) is on track to success in the collector's size of 1:87, with fans of the famous German comedians hankering after the Red-XXXXXXX-Killer (bottom).

Revell has now established itself as a supplier of military vehicles in the international scale of 1:35. In 2001, the MAN 10-ton 8x8 truck boosts the fleet of the East Westphalians.

2002

Dubbed the NSU TTS, Revell adds this brawny little guy to its program, which is launched on market as a 1:18 finished model sporting a variety of new race liveries.

Revell launched its "fascination model-making" campaign this year and clearly emphasized this in its catalog. The idea was also about making model-making interesting to a broader public. I was again involved mainly in new developments in the car sector, particularly in the die-cast segment. Once again we had illustrated the title of the catalog with a zinc die-cast model, the original of which would ultimately never go into mass production: it was the VW W12, a spectacular design from Wolfsburg that was unveiled to the public at the Tokyo Motor Show late in 2001. Thanks to our wonderful contact at Volkswagen, Klaus-Jürgen Glaser, we received all the documentation we needed and were even permitted to photograph the original. At this point in time, the plan was to produce the W12. However, the board made the decision to abandon this project and thus it died for us, as well. After all, we would only have been able to sell the required quantities if it had gone into production. Another concept was presented at Detroit in 2001 and realized by us: the VW Microbus, which was in fact a retro-car cross between a T1 and T2. As a large sedan it was supposed to fill the gap between the Sharan and T5. After we'd produced the model, VW decided that this car, too, would not go into production. If we'd received this information earlier, we would never have made this model. Positive news in the die-cast range was the launch of a series of racers based on the NSU-TT, a series that would run successfully for years.

Revell often uses spectacular new developments in aviation to come up with awesome kits. The new Airbus 380 makes its final approach. Revell miniaturizes this aircraft in the scale of 1:144 (bottom and right page).

Revell isn't afraid to take chances. In 2002, the Volkswagen concept for the new kombi, the Microbus, is created as a detailed zinc die-cast model. The downscaled model features moving doors, sliding doors and a hood that opens.

Revell has also made a name for itself amongst railway enthusiasts. The steam locomotive BR43 appears on the market as an intricate plastic model without a motor.

2003

Revell launches a new series of cars from the DTM race series as 1:32-scale Easy Kits. Shown here is the popular Audi TTS Hasseröder vehicle.

Once again I was kept busy this year with ship projects, where I designed the research vessel Meteor in conjunction with the Alfred Wegener Institute (AWI) in Bremerhaven. Since the original vessel spent most of the year in polar waters, I used a large shipyard model at the AWI as a template, and of course the necessary plans and drawings. Furthermore, Revell came up with a huge top seller with a sensational new development: a submarine Type VIIc in the super large scale of 1:72. The car fleet also grew significantly. For its research on the brand-new Ferrari Enzo, Revell got the measurements exclusively from Maranello and as a highlight also launched a large 1:12 model kit of the Ferrari F-2002. The innovative aspect of this kit was the pre-painted body parts. The red theme had become so popular at Revell that the manufacturer dedicated an entire double-spread to it in the catalog. Another innovation was the expansion of the Easy Kit series with vehicles from the German Touring Car Masters (DTM). Revell produced 1:32-scale kits for all the competing manufacturers; Mercedes, Audi and Opel. The research for all of these cars took place at Abt Sportsline in Kempten on the occasion of a one-day DTM exhibition. During negotiations with the licensing agency in Stuttgart, I had the pleasure of meeting Willy Weber, the manager of Michael and Ralf Schumacher. He owned the licensing agency. Over coffee and cake, we enjoyed a pleasant chat. I also caught up with Hans-Jürgen Abt, the boss of Abt Sportsline and the father the Abt-Audi TT DTM car. On this occasion, we produced a power point presentation of the entire new Easy Kit concept and we won him over. One of this year's new arrivals could only be seen undercover in the catalog: We had only just begun with the design and model development. It concerned construction machinery in the railway gauge "I" corresponding to a 1:32 scale. The entire line was realized in the lead-up with constructive

The series with the DTM racers carries the extra designation "multicolor", as the bodies are painted ex-works and come with additional decals.

The submarine Type VII as a large 1:72-scale U 552 is one of the flagship projects at Revell this year. The ready-made model measures almost 94 centimeters in length: a challenge for mold-making.

support from Michael Braig from the company Brami in Neuhausen. Michael with his undisputed expertise in the modeling profession helped me immensely in the development of this line. Unfortunately, the Chinese manufacturer of the kits filed for bankruptcy a few years later, while I was working on the next projects. With the insolvency, all of the tools were seized by the Chinese state. For this reason, we had to halt this very popular children's article.

Revell's cars are at full revs, too: For the slot-car track, the 1:32-scale Shelby Daytona Coupé is produced, and in the 1:18 scale, Revell recreates a Mercedes-Benz classic with the die-cast Ponton.

2004

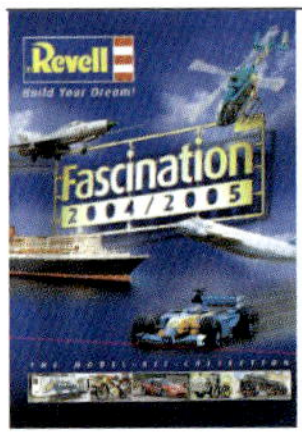

With the Easy Kits, Revell pursues a new idea in 2004: The Bünde team comes up with snap kits for 1:32-scale construction machinery with great playing features. Shown here is the Liebherr earthmover.

Again this year I had my hands full with an aircraft project. For years, a MiG 21 in a scale of 1:72 had been on the drawing board. More aircraft of this type were built after the Second World War than any other. As a basis, we used the original from the space exhibition in Morgenröthe: an F-13, a replica, incidentally, of the machine of the first German in space, Sigmund Jähn. This exhibition was built in honor of Jähn. Nowadays, we hold a model exhibition every two years in modern premises, at which our "Siggi" is the patron of the event. Since its popularity never waned after the 2004 premiere, the model was later reissued several times. This MiG 21 was definitely a landmark in Revell's aircraft projects. The die-cast area expanded to include an automobile from the GDR production, the widely popular Wartburg 311 in 1:18 made out of die-cast zinc. As developers at Revell, we enjoyed incredible support for this project from Michael Stück, the former director of customer services, who worked hard with support from BMW to uphold the Wartburg tradition after the end of the GDR. Thanks to Mike, we had access to all the planned 311 versions right through to the 313 Sport Coupe, the original of which is extremely rare. Slot cars, which were initiated by our American colleagues as 1:32 models for the slot-car track, were supplemented by our first in-house developments. Here, Revell once again put its faith in the NSU TT in several extra-wide racing variants: the Porsche 550 Spyder and a Jaguar E-Type Lightweight Coupé. The slot-racing series would expand the Revell range very successfully for several years.

The Russian MiG 21 F-13 takes off from the runway as a newly designed plastic kit in 1:72. The cockpit, suspension and armaments are authentically reproduced.

The transport giant Antonov An-121 (top) in a scale of 1:144 is another highlight of the year at Revell. The Fiat Abarth 1000 from 1965 (bottom) would send 1:18-scale die-cast model collectors into raptures.

Cars from Eastern Germany have enjoyed a long tradition at Bünde. Revell continues with this in 2004 with the most beautiful car from the former GDR. The template for this limited edition Wartburg 313 can be seen here with a hardtop and painted red.

2005

The modern search and rescue vessel Hermann Marwede in 1:72 is another feat of the East Westphalians and further expands the fleet for fans of plastic model kits.

Another plane project was on the drawing board for this year. The focus at Revell was to find an entirely new theme: the development of the first gliders in 1:32. Here, my excellent ties to the Bünde Aeroclub proved very helpful, whose originals have always provided the inspiration for our designs. We initially made an ASK 21. We still enjoy a close connection with the club today. The cooperation with the German Society for Shipwrecked Persons (DGzRS) was intensified in that Revell reproduced the Hermann Marwede in 1:72, the largest rescue vessel, which went into service in August 2003. And for this project, as well, the Revell team received exceptional support from the HQ in Bremen and from the crew on the island of Helgoland. Revell still enjoys close ties to the foreman Jörg Rabe and his crew. Thanks to my contact to Sinalco, I organized a special show truck for the truck sector. Our in-house designer, Andreas Metzner, created a Danish version of a refrigerated trailer in 1:24. Our Easy Kit construction machinery was flourishing. Revell planned to add three more sets including figurines and were also planning to add more of a play aspect. The bankruptcy of the Chinese manufacturer put a stop to this project. Moreover, the existing molds disappeared as part of the bankruptcy assets, which heralded a certain death for the series. The die-cast field, however, grew even more: this year with an Opel Kapitän, the Ford 17 M "Badewanne" (bathtub) and the Mercedes-Benz W 123 as a 1:18 sedan. Again with fantastic backing from Jürgen Lätsch from Hagen, the organizer of the NSU Berg Cup (hill-climb cup), I was able to expand the Berg Cup Series by two more vehicles, both limited editions, with the aim of reproducing the entire NSU starting grid. Ultimately, Revell achieved this. Furthermore, after the PV 544 Buckel, I wanted to create another Volvo: the Amazon. Revell received technical and material support from the Volvo expert Paul Uckelmann from Coesfeld. Without such people getting involved in these projects, developing vintage models would simply not

Revell pays tribute to the roadster of the small automobile manufacturer Wiesmann with a 1:18-model with a die-cast body and engine.

Gliders in 1:32 are a totally new idea. The range starts with the impressive ASK 21 Schleicher (top). For friends of automobile classics, Revell reproduces a 1:18 kit of the Swedish Volvo Amazon this year.

have been possible. The most interesting and adventurous development of this year was the Wiesmann Roadster. From the outset, I was involved with two people who lived and loved their product, the brothers Martin and Friedhelm Wiesmann. Wherever possible, these two helped me – Martin as an engineer and Friedhelm in sales. They dived into the project, taking care of the tiniest details, which resulted in an exquisite product. Over the years I witnessed the ongoing development of the brand, from the early days in Telgenkamp to its relocation to a new factory in Dülmen, where I eventually went on to develop the GT. Unfortunately, the production was eventually discontinued. The vehicles on the market are still sought-after gems and have appreciated significantly in value.

2006

In 2006, Revell celebrates its 50th anniversary and presents fans with a model of its own show truck with a Scania tractor unit and a colorfully designed three-axle semi-trailer as a 1:24 plastic kit.

In our 50th anniversary year, we experienced some very interesting encounters as part of our model developments. Existing contacts were revitalized with new projects, more gliders were created, the Ferrari theme boomed, another Volvo, the 1800 S, enhanced our 1:18 die-cast range and more NSU Berg Cup versions saw the light of day. Our shipping line would expand with another passenger vessel. For help with this, I contacted my old friend Henk Beentjes from IPMS, the plastic modelling association in the Netherlands, who got in touch with the Dutch Coast Guard. They put the former deep-sea tug Smit Houston into service as the coast guard boat under the name Waker. This collaboration worked brilliantly and we received super support, but unfortunately, several months after our model launch, an on-board fire put the Waker out of commission. The damages were irreparable and the ship had to be scrapped. I'll always remember the customary model presentation on board the Waker in Den Helder with my old friend Henk Beentjes, who sadly passed away much too early. For the anniversary, I had the job of organizing a very special event: On the occasion of our 50-year anniversary, Revell wanted to create its own show truck. As far as I was concerned, there was only one person who could do this and that was the show-truck airbrush specialist Walter Rosner. He had already designed quite a few of these trucks, all of which were distributed by Herpa in a 1:87 scale. Via my mate Matthias Wolff from Herpa, I managed to tee-up a meeting with Walter Rosner to give him the brief. He then found us a suitable freight forwarder on whose semi-trailer we wanted to transfer our design. After several weeks, just in time for the big Revell anniversary celebration in the Gerry Weber Event Center, the giant rolling jewel was ready. We positioned the truck out in the open. It was a real eye-catcher and many photographs were taken of it. Obviously we then turned the original into a model kit, but we used a Scania as the tractor unit because,

Revell builds a 1:18 ready-made model of Simon Templar's Volvo 1800 S in beige with a red interior.

A new harbor tug is needed. The Smit Houston proves to be the prototype for Revell to create an authentic-looking plastic kit in 1:144 in its anniversary year.

at the time of developing the model, we didn't really know which tractor unit would be used. Herpa actually launched the model with the correct Mercedes Actros as the hauler. A small number of these were put into Revell packaging and are still a very popular gift for special visitors to Revell.

More and more, Revell's NSU TTS turns into a hot favorite: no matter if it's a slot racer for the track in 1:32 or, as shown here, a die-cast 1:18-model with opening doors and engine hood. Something else becomes apparent in 2006: the models should have nice and wide fenders, rims and tires.

2007

The strategists come up with another head-turner for the finished 1:18 classics: The first generation Volkswagen Scirocco serves as the basis for a top quality die-cast zinc model.

Technological advances dominated the 2007 catalog: Revell underlined this by declaring that all of its new products were produced using 100 percent CAD technology, or in other words, created using computer-aided design. We'd been working with CAD since the early days of our collaboration with Heljan in Denmark, but we would still occasionally develop products in the conventional way. However, by the year 2000 we'd switched exclusively to applying this technology to designing our models. At the same time, I'd withdrawn more and more from the actual designing of individual products and left that job to my project managers. But I was still very interested in all new products, after all, I was ultimately responsible for these models, especially when it came to the financial and time-management aspects. During this year a decision was made, without a lot of meetings and calculations, to produce a plastic model kit of the new Audi R8. When this latest development with the four rings was picked up by the press for the first time, it became immediately clear that Revell would add this spectacular sports car to its range as a 1:24 model. Our excellent connection to Audi, which had grown over the years, greatly assisted us in that we received the necessary technical information at an early stage. Only then can a good model emerge. Heeding the many requests from our customers, we introduced another new product: a fire engine in 1:24. The partner for this project was the company Schlingmann in Dissen. Our contact there was Mr. Beckmann, and he lent us great support. First we produced three different versions based on a Mercedes chassis, which can now be purchased on a MAN chassis. We added another vintage car to our die-cast range with the DKW Junior, as well as a modern classic, the VW Scirocco I. The Volkswagen Scirocco in particular showed that a manufacturer shouldn't always listen to the ardent wishes of its customers, because, despite its different color versions, the classic coupé from Lower Saxony was ultimately not a big success economically.

The illustration alone of the new Schlingmann fire engine in 1:24 whets fans appetite for more: Revell again invests in another emergency vehicle with a top finish.

The large image at the top shows the extent of Revell's detailing behind the roll-up doors of the Schlingmann HLF 16-20. And, of course, the kit also comes with a hose reel. In close cooperation with Audi, Revell launches a kit of the R8 super sports car as a coupé in 2007.

The product development department is always finding originals that promise lucrative production runs to turn into 1:18-scale finished models. In 2007, work on the Opel Manta 400i begins – a handmade sample is pictured below. Over the course of its evolution as a Revell miniature, an authentic racing version eventually arrives.

2008

With the German army's light Wolf military vehicle, the company from Bünde expands its kit range in the military scale of 1:35. Revell also works meticulously on the all-wheel-drive detailing.

This year marked the start of a phase in which I began to delegate projects and only helped my colleagues with certain products. One of these was the Neoplan Cityliner N1216HD, which was definitely a kind of flagship project for Revell as a 1:24 kit. I was able to accompany and assist the project manager, Daniel Pasternok, several times and provide operational support. The Waker of the Dutch Coast Guard, which had been proposed the previous year, now appeared on store shelves. And, as I'd suggested long ago, we finally delivered one of the most famous military vehicles without armor, chains or weaponry: The Wolf. During research, we were again able to use our great contacts to the Bundeswehr base at Augustdorf. The 1:18 metal line expanded to include the Opel Manta 400 and Mercedes-Benz 450 SEL of the W116 series. For my part, I got the chance to take on a new adventure on behalf of Revell. The original came from an idea of Klaus-Dieter Frers, the CEO of the supplier Paragon and owner of the new car make Artega. The Artega GT was to be the first composite construction model. This meant that the body was made of painted plastic, with the chassis and other components consisting of die-cast zinc. We jumped to the task. This made Revell the first company to have realized a 1:18 model following this technological layout. Working with Klaus-Dieter Frers was extremely pleasant. As an avid model collector himself, he knew what to place value on. The full size Artega GT had all the makings of a commercial success, but unfortunately didn't have the right investors on board. Just several years after opening, the company was declared bankrupt. Klaus-Dieter Frers, however, eventually bought the entire property back for Paragon as a test lab.

Revell adds the colorful coast guard boat Waker to its 2008 range. It is indeed astonishing how much detailing today's modern small 1:1200-scale plastic kits offer.

Revell comes up with two innovations. The Neoplan Cityliner in 1:24 (top), a major project for the commercial vehicle range which is developed in close cooperation with the bus manufacturer. The interior fit-out represents a model-making masterpiece. And in the 1:18-scale, Revell is the first supplier to use composite construction with its Artega GT. From this point on, the bodies of its finished models are made of plastic instead of die-cast zinc.

2009

In 1959 the 1:25 VW Microbus appears in the USA. Now the crew at Bünde introduces a completely redesigned plastic model in 1:24, which is unparalleled in its detailing and moving parts.

This year's catalog was packed with new items in almost every product category, with the 40th anniversary of the moon landing playing a special role. For this event, Revell obviously revived some of its classic models. And this is bound to happen again on the occasion of the moon landing's 50th anniversary in 2019. The highlight in the plastic kit line was without doubt the Colombo Express container ship in 1:700. A little comment on the side: Due to the detailed licensing agreement with Hapag-Lloyd, we were only allowed to "load" our kit with Hapag-Lloyd containers. Looking back, this turned out to be a big mistake, as the box illustrations and the advertisement appeared bland and were at odds with reality. Right from the start, the VW Samba bus has been synonymous with the Revell name, the original mold of which unfortunately underwent an irreversible redesign in the early sixties by Revell USA. This made a reissue of the original Samba on the basis of the original model impossible. Thus, Revell made the brave decision to design a completely new VW T1 Samba using the latest tool technology. For the sake of nostalgia, the body was made up of individual components, as it was in the sixties. The kit was a hit. This year Germany also celebrated the 20th anniversary of the fall of the Berlin wall. On this occasion, we decided to reconstruct the "Trabi", which had enjoyed success for 20 years, but this time using the latest technology. Unlike the first kit, which featured a simple design due to time constraints, the new model should be particularly sophisticated and we pulled out all stops when it came to modern mold-making. And so it came to be. At an anniversary event, the new Trabi was unveiled. But there's more: on the occasion of the "model hobby spiel" at Leipzig in 2009, Revell had an original decorated by graffiti artists with the theme "20 Years after the fall of the wall". The PR partner for this project was Wolfgang Stumph, the main character in the movie *Go, Trabi, Go*. "Stumpi" and the former President of the German Cancer Aid gave the go-ahead for a then-popular auction with proceeds going to the non-profit organization. With the new development, we undertook very different and significantly more detailed research. Starting with the in-house creation of 3D data of the original, all details could now be researched and measured with much more precision. The managing director of our licensing partner Intertrab in Zwickau, Wolfgang Kießling, and the well-known Trabi specialist Bert Oehlgardt from Bad Köstritz, gave us support with this job. What emerged was an exceptionally detailed model symbolizing the reunification and a history-maker based on a car "made in the GDR".

You first have to come up with such an idea: Revell launches a huge container ship. Despite its 1:700 scale, the vessel is almost 48 centimeters long. Moreover, it's a year of anniversaries: with the 1:24 Trabant kit, Revell commemorates 20 Years since the fall of the Berlin wall.

Take me to the moon: 40 years after the moon landing is another occasion for many new products emerging from the well-stocked mold pool at Revell. The image on the right shows the fitting logo, at the bottom is the intricate lunar module in a scale of 1:48.

2010

Made from new molds, Revell puts the legendary German battleship, the Bismarck, into the limelight as a plastic kit in 2010. Despite its compact 1:700 scale, the intricate ship superstructures are authentically portrayed. The finished model measures almost 36 centimeters in length.

This was a year of major projects that were both interesting and challenging. For Revell's new model year, a whole series of History Makers were created, representing milestones such as the three great aircraft models in the large 1:32-scale: the Heinkel He 111, the Arado Ar 196 and die BAe Hawk. The ship segment in the range was buoyed by incredibly detailed Bismarck and Tirpitz kits in 1:350, created following brand-new documents. Revell also dived deeper into the world of the DTM, or the German Touring Car Masters. Not as a 1:32 model, but now again in the classic 1:24-car scale and of course with rafts of additional details. Also joining the range this year was the current touring car racer from Mercedes-Benz and Audi, including realistic decals for a prototypical livery. And, 2010 yielded yet another absolutely top secret car, a vehicle that we weren't even allowed to show in our catalog, a spectacular new sports car: the Mercedes SLS AMG. Our military ranks expanded, this time with a new recruit from the German army in the form of the Wiesel. Our in-house die-cast line was temporarily discontinued due to the extremely high manufacturing costs in China. In order to sell the necessary quantities, Revell had to achieve certain target prices. This was becoming increasingly more difficult in view of the increase in costs for labor and, above all, raw materials and energy. In order to continue offering die-cast models, Revell Germany found a substitute and joined forces with the producers of the 1:18-line Shelby Collectibles and took these vehicles into its program to sell. The "Berlin Wall Trabi" that I created with the Leipzig Graffiti Community came out in a limited special edition as a 1:24 kit. Again, all proceeds went to the German Cancer Aid. In this year, our new pillar Revell-Control appeared on store shelves for the first time featuring a small radio control program for beginners. Over the next years, this program would turn into a huge hit. This represents an additional mainstay for Revell and is gaining in importance today.

Revell puts its faith in the revived DTM with 1:24 kits. In addition to the Audi A4, the team from Bünde accurately depicts the C class from Mercedes-Benz in plastic.

Revell isn't afraid to try new materials. The developers from Bünde made the 1:48-model of Leonardo da Vinci's "airscrew" almost entirely from laser-cut wood – a real pioneering feat.

The completely redeveloped Arado Ar 196 in a scale of 1:32 displays incredible detailing right through to the folding wings. Another newcomer to the Revell range in this scale is the colorful BAe Hawk of the Red Arrows.

2011

The Neoplan obviously gives a taste for more: Revell launches its second 1:24 bus as a kit, the classic London double-decker.

One of the big topics for this year was the new Airbus A400M military transporter, which was considerably easier to come by in 1:72 at Revell than the original. These were joined by other novelties, the Lynx Navy helicopter in 1:32, the legendary sailing ship Wasa in 1:150, the new AIDAdiva in the large 1:400 scale based on the real ship built in the Meyer shipyard at Papenburg, and a classic London double-decker bus in 1:24 – a real giant with twin tires at the rear. As a sideline of our large Marwede from the German Society for the Rescue of Shipwrecked Persons, a miniaturized 1:200 version was developed for enthusiastic beginners. In the car segment, we added a Citroen 2CV to the modern classic range, with an Audi R8 Spyder joining the modern car fleet. Both kits came in 1:24. The Star Wars theme was growing and gaining more importance at Revell. One of my tasks this year was to take on a brand new project: historical inventions of Leonardo Da Vinci using a wooden construction with individual laser-cut parts, everything ready to assemble as a kit using wood glue, all packaged attractively and with nice gimmicks as an extra. Initially I made ten kits, all in exclusive collaboration with the Milan National Museum, home to a large Leonardo exhibition with models of his inventions. I measured and photographed these model myself, with my friend from Rome, Mario Falconi, producing the kit designs. He prepared the CAD data for the laser. This was a completely new technology which made it possible for us to create new products without having to make molds in the conventional way. This new series proved hugely popular, especially amongst museums, schools and young people. In a now separate catalog, other products were offered such as the Mag Clicks pearl series, a horse range and other products specifically targeted at female customers.

Dream ships are a big theme for Revell. In 2011, the AIDAdiva in 1:400 weighs anchor and heads off to cruise the oceans of the world. This is a range with a lot of wind in its sails.

Sometimes Revell kits outpace reality. While the real Airbus A400M military transporter is still grounded, the 1:72 is already airborne.

Revell also offers the Hermann Marwede in smaller sizes – 1:200 (top). This compact kit of the Sea Rescue boat will turn into a success. While the paintwork on the Westland Lynx (bottom) of the German Airforce impresses, the interior of 1:32 kit also delights: note the meticulous interior features and the intricate rotor blades.

2012

A real challenge for aircraft fans is the 1:32 kit of the Heinkel He 219 A-7 with its delicate antennas on Revell's night fighter version.

Revell once again offered a handful of real highlights this year. These included the large 1:32-scale Messerschmitt Me 109 and Heinkel He 219 aircraft, which were extremely well received by modelers. That this scale was gaining in popularity was due to the fact that these models featured even the tiniest details. In the 1:700 scale, Revell lays the foundation for a completely redeveloped Titanic, this too following the latest findings from underwater investigations. With two new Ferrari, the 599 GTO and the SA Aperta, this theme shifted up a gear. In addition and as a complement to our vintage cars, a classic Mini Cooper joined the fleet. All car kits made their debut this year in the top-selling 1:24 scale. A new vehicle from the German Armed Forces, the so-called SPz Puma, was created in 1:35 in close cooperation with the manufacturer and the Ministry of Defense. I expanded the series of Leonardo kits with two more products, again in collaboration with the Milan Museum, this time, however, de Vinci's weapon inventions, as specifically requested by the public. Both were produced as kits with laser-cut wood components. The area of die-cast and slot cars only appeared in the catalog as a side note. This year, a decision was reached to no longer invest in this product group for the time being, but to only produce the occasional small run of individual types and then illustrate them in the catalog. We continued in this way until the end of 2014. The prices continued to spiral upwards, which was no longer acceptable.

Despite its gray appearance, the classic Mini as a 1:24 kit from Revell is anything but mousy. The fine detailing on the plastic kit shows the cutting-edge technology of the British compact car classic. The kit also includes the authentically reproduced transversally mounted four-cylinder engine and steerable front wheels.

The Titanic is always a popular topic for a plastic kit set. Shown here above is the 1:700 kit from Revell with its intricate deck design. Moreover, Revell also brings out a new aircraft in 1:32 (bottom). The Messerschmitt Bf-109 takes off in the new G-6 version.

For modelers who enjoy assembling the latest military vehicles from the German Armed Forces, Revell offers something new for 2012. The SPz Puma makes its debut as a plastic kit in what is arguably the world's most widely used 1:35 scale.

2013

The DTM heads into its next round at Revell with the latest racers lining up on the grid as plastic kits in the 1:24 scale. Shown here is the BMW M3 from 2013 in very fine detail.

This year, Revell once again got a new owner, the company Hobbico from the USA. I was used to this, after all, I'd "survived" all seven Revell owners up until this time. You eventually get accustomed to such things. Here's the background: Hobbico, particularly renowned in the field of RC products, needed Revell to get access into the European market. With its excellent pan-European sales network, Revell was the obvious choice. On top of this, of course, they would have a certain new influence on the product policy. The plastic kits would remain as the mainstay of the program, for which we would continue to be autonomously responsible, but the remote control products were to be expanded. Importantly, over the years, the American Revell range had pulled farther and farther away from our European program, allegedly due to the entirely different needs in the markets. Hence, it always surprised me how well our new "German" products were received in the original German boxes in the USA and how they supplemented their program. But Americans were always a mystery to me. We'd rigorously followed our own product policy over the years, while the USA had moved more and more towards easy self-assembly kits and beginner models. Much to our regret. Revell at Bünde had indeed considered beginners, but had still looked after advanced modelers with flagship projects, which ultimately became pivotal for the image of the company. In 2013, for example, we again came up with new developments in all product areas and launched real winners on the market. 1:32 aircraft kits were in vogue, a 1:48 Tornado set new quality standards, but was pitched to the market decidedly too cheap. The cruise ship segment was expanded with two Norwegian Hurtigruten ships, and the next IX C U-boat in the super 1:72 scale appeared. The car category was bolstered by a DTM BMW and Sebastian Vettel's Formula One Red Bull, and a brand-new VW Beetle in 1:24 was added to the vintage range. The military ranks continued to enjoy a high level of popularity, however models based on World War One lost all importance. Vehicle and aircraft from the Second World War were also in a nosedive. In demand this year were kits of current models.

The elaborate illustration on the box shows the original ship ploughing through tempestuous seas. Revell builds the IX C U-boat in 1:27. The original ship went to sea for the first time in 1938.

It drove its way into the hearts of millions of drivers and hence was a must as a 1:24 kit at Revell: the VW Beetle (top) with its intricate model engine. Sporting a truly “devilish” livery, the Tornado IDS (bottom left) joins the 1:48 fleet of plastic model kits. By contrast, the Hurtigruten line is represented in the 1:200 scale at Revell by a plastic miniature of the Trollfjord, which fans of the kit brand eagerly assemble.

2014

As a result of rigorous product streamlining, the 2014 catalog had only 102 pages. Nevertheless, Revell brought out interesting new products in all important areas of the program without having to strain the budget. The aircraft area continued to be dominated by kits in the scale of 1:72 and 1:32, an example of which was the spectacular new development, the 1:32 Spitfire. And civil aviation was also growing in popularity, and this, of course, had an impact on novelties. After many years, the space theme was revisited, with the arrival of the Space Ship Two from Virgin Galactic (1:144). By popular request and as a novelty in the increasingly attractive shipping sector, Revell developed a modern harbor tug, the Fairplay in 1:144. Furthermore, the military ship range was enhanced by a landing craft based on an early German army model, again in 1:144. 2014 was another anniversary year: namely, 25 years since the fall of the Berlin wall. For this, we considered developing another Trabant, this time based on the new 601 S, the Universal, which was a hatchback version of the "Trabi". Here, too, I was lucky enough to have backing from specialists in this field, Wolfgang Kießling from Intertrab and Bert Oehlgardt, the "Trabi" expert without equal. What emerged was another incredibly detailed, completely new 1:24 kit that was unparalleled. For the Leipzig Model Hobby Games held in early October of this year, Revell again displayed another original designed by the Leipzig graffiti community. After the toy fair, this 1:1 original was again auctioned online and the proceeds went to Children's Cancer Aid. Unfortunately, the car didn't fetch the sum we'd hoped for. Another car novelty made its debut in the Revell program alongside the "Trabi"; the La Ferrari in 1:24. The modern classic line was enhanced by a VW Golf I, closed and open and both in 1:24. In the military sector, the 1:72-scale was gaining in popularity, and this was reflected in the model range.

As a Boeing 747-8F cargo plane, Revell launches the Jumbo as a plastic model kit now in a scale of 1:144.

The “strawberry basket” finally arrives in craft shops in a 1:24 kit. This Revell kit marks the first edition of the open Golf from Karmann as an authentically recreated miniature.

Revell at Bünde places a great deal of value on its illustrations. This is apparent in the drawing of the Cargo Jumbo (bottom) as well as the photorealistic illustration of the Space-Ship Two, which debuts as a 1:144 kit.

2015

The year 2015 was again packed with surprises in terms of new products. A spectacular addition to the aircraft fleet was the C-54 Skymaster (Raisin Bomber) in 1:72 with almost 400 individual parts. More novelties also joined the aircraft and helicopter range. In the ship armada, we modified the existing Hermann Marwede in 1:72 on the occasion of the "150 Years of Sea Rescue Service" celebrations by adding a new auxiliary boat with an outboard engine. The original model had a couple of kinks that had occurred during the development stage, which we then had to iron out. In the car branch, we made the attempt to launch a multi-window Samba bus in the large 1:16-scale on the market – with success. The political discussions around electric mobility bore fruit at Revell with the 1:24-scale BMWi8. And in the truck fleet, we put the Schlingmann fire-engine series on MAN chassis, as the licensing talks with Mercedes simply weren't much fun anymore. In the military program, Revell focused on more modern construction designs in the two model kit scales of 1:72 and 1:35, with the Bundeswehr topic gaining more and more traction. Particularly spectacular was the new development of the Leopard 1 on a large 1:35 scale.

2015 is another year for the automobile, as underscored by these two 1:24 kits. The bottom left image shows the MAN TGM Schlingmann as a HLF 20. At the bottom right is a photo of the hybrid BMW i8 kit. The developers of this miniature put a great deal of value on reproducing the sophisticated drivetrain of the coupé.

On land and in the air: The model illustrated at the top can be assembled into a 1:72-scale model of the Douglas C-54 Skymaster. Below, the fitting illustration of the large 1:16-scale VW Kombi.

On water: Revell also remains true to Sea Rescue vessels and delivers a modified version of the Hermann Marwede in 1:72, where it attracts great interest.

2016

Nicknamed “the duck” in Germany, the 1:24 kit of the Citroen 2CV compact car appears in stores with matching decals.

After huge celebrations on the occasion of Revell’s 50th anniversary in 2006, no official celebrations were expected for the company’s 60th birthday. In the previous year, the product developers had come together to discuss several fundamental measures that were long overdue. First amongst ourselves, then finally as an innovation team to the management, we proposed to revamp our product strategy. Instead of categorizing the products according to skill levels, which were somewhat incomprehensible to the average modeler, we wanted to find a suitable system for grading the level of difficulty for our kits. The important thing with this: the program should put more emphasis on young customers, for which Revell, after a great deal of effort, launched the brand-new pre-school “Junior” range. This has established itself as a successful program and a top seller until today. At last we had kits that were literally child’s play to assemble. The new classifications of the kits now worked on levels, a term that came from the world of computer games and was easy to understand. Kits were developed according to these different levels. And as the greatest innovation, we also wanted to completely upgrade and modernize our assembly instructions, which were then printed in four colors. The individual construction stages were easier to understand and came with few parts. This made everything more transparent. This measure was the brainchild of product development. The marketing people took over the baton, and, a year later, were able to show the first results. All of these measures have so far been extremely well received by the market. For Revell, it marked an important strategic step into the future of the company. It’s strange that our American colleagues didn’t adopt this new system, and instead opted to stick with the old regime. Conspicuous in the 2016 catalog: not one Ferrari is included. Why? Shortly before the catalog went to print, Maranello retracted its license agreement with Revell. The reason given was that model kits were apparently no longer a suitable fit for the Ferrari portfolio. This seemed somewhat hard to believe, since other kit providers continued to build licensed models based on these red cars. Unfortunately, all further efforts to prevent this failed. However, on a positive note, we received a request via our internet homepage asking if we were keen to develop a new helicopter from the KSK (Special Forces Command) of the German Armed Forces parallel to the original. Since Revell already had the basis model of the helicopter line in its program, we decided to go ahead with the project. Those responsible at the KSK and the manufacturer of Airbus Helicopters supported us as much as they could. The scheduled delivery date, however, could not be kept, as we had to make significantly more changes to the special 1:32-scale helicopter than were originally planned. Another interesting novelty was a BMW Isetta as a plastic kit in the scale of 1:16. Here, a 1:12 Isetta kit from the com-

Car kits with a difference: Revell launches its Junior Kits series for very young modelers and sets a benchmark. In the best sense conventional but no less successful is the 1:16 kit of the BMW Isetta.

pany Premium Classixxs stood us in good stead. The 1:12 Isetta from this company, which was founded in 2002, was originally my initiative because I had close ties to the two company founders. 2016 was also the year I started my own club, the "Bünde Friends of Model-Making". Shortly before my retirement, I was able to organize the first model construction exhibition in support of the German Children's Cancer Aid in Bünde. 2,500 visitors came and we collected a donation of almost 10,000 Euro. For a premiere, this result was a huge success.

2017

In 2017, helicopter fans can look forward to the Airbus-Helicopter H145M in 1:32, which from a technical research point of view was big challenge for Revell. The model is impressive right down to the detailing.

After the very successful launch of the new Junior line, a whole raft of models and themes were introduced into the program. In addition, other licensing themes such as *Star Wars, Halo, Cars* and *Star Trek* were developed specifically for the younger target group. A sensational new addition to the aircraft segment was a 1:48 Bristol Beaufighter and a brand-new 1:32 P-51 Mustang. In the sailing ship sector, the Black Pearl from the *Pirates of the Caribbean* appeared in two scales, 1:72 and 1:150. After fielding many requests, Revell developed a completely new PT-109 patrol torpedo boat in a scale of 1:72 and two new Porsche 934 RSR and a Panamera in 1:24 joined the fleet of cars. Truly sensational, however, and after years of discussions, we finally brought out the first Revell tractor as a Porsche Junior 108 in the collector's scale of 1:24. Success was guaranteed. I experienced my first model year as a retiree working as a so-called "consultant". This meant that I still worked for Revell on a daily basis and I was responsible for answering all sorts of letters and correspondence from the service department and for the input of our online customers. There were many queries that required a certain historical understanding of Revell and I tried to answer these as competently as possible. I received a lot of very positive feedback and I'm now in private contact with many modelers, international ones as well. In 2018 I will celebrate my 50th anniversary at Revell, which will be held on the occasion of the 2nd model-making exhibition at Bünde for the benefit of the German Children's Cancer Aid. I'll continue with designing products, but only privately, and leave the respective sales to other companies, Revell for instance. I still have plenty of ideas up my sleeve, ideas that I was never able nor permitted to realize during my time at Revell, but the success of which I am totally convinced. My experience from all my years at Revell and in the model markets gives me this certitude.

The 1:32 kit of the EMPI Imp dune buggy is reissued on the basis of an old Snap Fit mold – this time with decals.

The KSK helicopter is shown below. Above, a Revell model kit sets another milestone in red: With the Porsche Junior, the East Westphalians launch the Easy Click series.

While the red Porsche tractor is kept as a 1:24 kit, the yellow and black Corvette racer is developed in the U.S. in the popular 1:25-scale mounted with a V8 engine.

2018

Revell makes men: For the Junior kits, Revell begins producing small figurines. Aside from civilian figures, Revell also sells firemen and more.

When Revell starts something, the East Westphalians don't stop until it's properly finished. In January, the firm produced the VW Beetle with working lights in 1:16 as the first model of the Revell technical series, followed by the Junkers Ju 88 in 1:32 and the Flower Class Corvette in 1:72 – all three featuring electronic lighting. More is to come. Thanks to the successful Junior kits, Revell headed into a new era: With the Porsche 911 Coupé, Targa and "Polizei" the first kits appeared based on a "real" model. Even Zuffenhausen had expressed this wish. More Junior kits from the movie Cars bolstered the range. Science fiction fans were treated to new products from the *Star Wars* sequel *The Last Jedi*; the Imperial Star Destroyer in 1:4000 and the A-Wing-Fighter in 1:44. In the widest sense of the science fiction topic but from the past, the German Haunebu-type flying saucer from the forties was introduced in 1:72. The Easy Click series, which can be assembled without glue thanks to clever snap connections, was expanded once again. The 2017 Ford GT in 1:24 and a new 1:16 Porsche 356 as a coupé joined the fleet. Revell Germany plans to produce a matching convertible of the 356, but as a top level 4 kit in 1:16. In this same scale, the East Westphalians converted the kombi from a bus to a transporter. For truck fans, Revell introduced the Mercedes Actros MP4 in 1:24. As incredibly intricate kits, 2018 brought aircraft enthusiasts the Heinkel He 177

On the occasion of the Football World Cup in Russia in 2018, Revell brings out a mini football as a co-axial rotor helicopter with radio remote control and flag design. The Flower Class Corvette comes as an electronic kit in the technology series.

Stars Wars adventurer Han Solo and his shaggy co-pilot Chewbacca fly through the galaxies in 1:72 thanks to Revell. In contrast, the 1:32 H-145 Helicopter seems terrestrial. That, however, seems almost unfair, because the details of the plastic kit from East Westphalia really deserve the name celestial.

"Greif" in 1:72, and the Bristol Beaufighter made its debut in 1:48. The mighty Antonov AN-225 extended the 1:144-scale fleet. Modeling captains can get on board with the Verena, a search and rescue ship for the Marwede in 1:72, the USS Hornet CV-8 in 1:1200 and the Corvette HMS Buttercup in 1:144. Moreover, Revell revved up its motorbike range in 1:8. In addition to two U.S. bikes, the BMW R75/5 once again took the stage as a reissue. This motorcycle model had been the first kit developed out of Bünde. In the RC program of Revell-Control, monster cars were planned as well as the 1:24-scale BMW X6 »Police«, a road and a U.S. police version of the Lamborghini Aventador. The in-house drone program featured increasingly compact and well equipped units, with better cameras as well as light functions. Revell combined the Quadrocopter with glasses, giving pilots the feeling they are flying on board the drone.

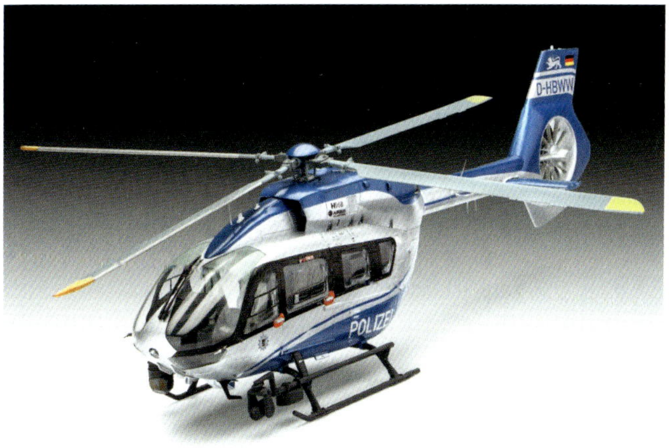

20...

Revell with a cause

Not even the recent change of ownership can throw Revell off-track – and that's a good thing!

It is this masterful balance between experimentation on the one hand and tradition on the other that distinguished Revell, especially Revell GmbH in Bünde, from all other companies in the toy industry. Not even the announcements that had caused tremors since April 2018 could rock this solid company. The current Revell owner, Hobbico from Illinois, filed for "Chapter 11" bankruptcy. Immediately, rumors spread that Revell would more than likely be sold. But why?

Small experiments: The Isetta is an example of how Revell works. When it becomes evident that the 1:18 market is booming, Revell comes up with an idea that no one else has: small cars from the economic boom era.

Granted, an American company under Chapter 11 needs to sell off assets to pay its creditors. And, Revell was extremely attractive, a veritable T-bone steak in Hobbico ownership – and one weighing at least 850 grams.

The sale of Revell GmbH in Bünde to the Munich-based financial investment company Quantum Capital Partners may even represent a great chance in the long term for the Bünde branch. After all, it wouldn't affect the current business. Moreover, it shows that the new investor wants to strengthen the position of managing director Stefan Krings. The balance of power in the future is weighted more towards Bünde than the United States. And Krings could succeed in what his predecessors Heinz-Georg Schöneberg, Kurt Haubrok and Hans Ullrich Remfert also achieved: to herald in a new era at the model kit company in East Westphalia.

Revell underlined just how innovative it is with the junior kit series launched several years previously. Customers snapped up 750,000 of these kits in a very short time. What's more, with these kits, Revell cultivates the model builders of tomorrow and sets new benchmarks in the field of budding hobbyists. The first junior kit based on a real original, the Porsche 911, will further expand this new mainstay and boost the appeal. This represents the sales "turbo" for the junior kits.

Revell with a cause: As long as slot-car racing was a hot topic, Revell creates collectible treasures like this limited-edition 1:32-scale James Dean Spyder. Later, they put on the brakes.

The success story of the courageous German company is also thanks a second successful niche, the in-house RC range, which with its dynamism can win new customers for the brand. Revell also learned from its own history. In radio-controlled models, the supply of spare parts adds to the successful image. Decades of data gleaned from the tried-and-true Department "X" for the plastic kitmakers could bear fruit here in another area.

The chronology that we've outlined in this book shows very clearly that Revell in Bünde was undoubtedly the more creative location. The reason for this is that company had to supply all of Europe. And the more they focussed on the interests of customers from the Netherlands, France, England and Co., the more the business flourished. The Kickomania football figures are examples of this innovation. Did Revell USA offer its customers key players from the American Football League? Revell Germany also knew when to pull the plug on experiments at the right time. When the diecast market and slot-car sales weakened, Bünde pulled the pin.

Nevertheless, there are, of course, important tasks for the future. If Stefan Krings manages to open a new chapter and find another pillar for the company to rest on, he may leave a lasting legacy in the history of Revell. I wish the team the best of luck in their endeavors!

Andreas A. Berse

Vorsprung durch friendship

Audi and Revell have at times rocked the model-car scene – thanks as well to the friendship between Thomas Frank and Ulli Taubert.

When Thomas Frank moved from BMW to Audi in 1991 he couldn't possibly have imagined that the Ingolstädt enterprise today would own a brilliant museum and have built a department called Audi Tradition that thrills fans with spectacular classics. As the long-standing head of Audi Tradition, Frank just may have had something to do with this: "Audi was eager to shake things up, to shuck off its old-fashioned image. There was a real sense of optimism in the air." Frank received exciting tasks: responsible for the marketing of the mid-engine Audi quattro Spyder sports cars, he earned his first laurels.

He was then handed another assignment as part of his function by the model-car fan Franz-Josef Paefgen, who at that time was responsible for product planning at Audi. His job: model cars and their marketing. Thomas Frank: "We'd already established something along these lines at BMW. The quality of the 1:87 models from Rietze and the 1:43 and 1:24 Schabak miniatures at Audi in 1991 fluctuated greatly. I wanted to squeeze more out of this theme." A spectacular Audi showcar, which was unveiled at the Tokyo Motor Show in 1991, presented him with the opportunity: the Audi Avus quattro.

Enter Ulli Taubert. The development man at Revell wanted to raise the profile of the diecast newcomers from Bünde with slightly different 1:18 models. This proved serendipitous for both parties. Frank's job at Audi was to market the special Avus quattro project. His goal: to create a 1:18 model of the fully chrome-plated concept. Frank even made sure that Revell was permitted to exhibit the original car at its novelty presentation in Bad Soden. This, too, was a premiere for Audi.

The first encounter left its mark: "I was immediately impressed by the commitment, the knowledge, and by Ulli Taubert himself. What's more, Revell was already an internationally known brand." For Audi, a 1:18 Avus was put on a glossy pedestal in Audi packaging. The 4,000 units sold out in record time and have now become sought-after collectors' items. They cost 69 deutschmarks each at that time. The No. 0001 from this series hand-signed by Ulli Taubert sits on Thomas Frank's desk at home. The man from the company with four rings: "This model goes with me whenever I move; I'll never let that one go."

Later, when Thomas Frank took over the role at Audi Tradition and wanted to position the brand history of Audi, including Horch, DKW, Wanderer, NSU and Auto Union, in the collector shelves, Revell kept the pace at full revs. The "stromlinie" of Auto Union, the DKW 1000 S Coupé, the first Audi TT and the NSU TTS evolved in 1:18 – the latter also as a slot-car racer in 1:32. Moreover, Revell at Bünde brought out several DTM racers with the four rings on the radiator

Lords of the Rings: Ulli Taubert from Revell (left) hands Thomas Frank from Audi Tradition the fully chrome-plated tooling model of the Audi Avus quattro. Both have enjoyed a long-standing friendship, from which many successful projects have emerged.

in 1:32 and 1:24. The Avus quattro even appeared as a plastic model in 1:43 with movable doors. Frank had successfully made the diversity of Audi history into a forte and this also worked with the fascination of model cars: starting with the spectacular vehicles from Horch and the racers from Auto Union.

During the many years of working alongside Ulli Taubert, a friendship grew that went beyond a mere business relationship. This is why the tooling model of the chrome-plated version of the Audi Avus has a very special place in Frank's office. "For me, it represents a milestone in our collaboration. Ulli presented it to me during his first model-kit exhibition at Bünde. It was an emotional moment for me." When talking about Taubert, the man from Ingolstadt is full of praise: "He's a cheerful northern German guy with an open face and a model-car mind. And, he does his job with a great deal of passion, he's committed to the company, and he does his best to make things happen. We'll stay in touch for the rest of our lives. I have a very high regard for this friendship. Taubert lives for what he does."

Friends help each other, as well. Due to the complicated galvanization process, there was a great deal of waste in the production of the fully chromed body. Therefore, as an exception, Revell got permission to offer the Audi Avus in black and white, despite the fact that it didn't exist. Thomas Frank: "Even when Taubert and I go into retirement, we'll always keep in touch. That's a matter of honor."

Andreas A. Berse

Remote-controlled success

For the last ten years, Revell-Control has been a lucrative mainstay of the brand. But, remote-controlled models are not something new.

Even before the Bünde team launched Revell-Control exactly twenty years ago, Revell Germany already offered remote control models. In 2004, for example, they created car bodies out of a plastic kit from Mercedes, Audi and Opel from the DTM, as well as Citroen, Peugeot and Subaru from the WRC in 1:32 and mini trucks in 1:87. Revell sold over 50,000 units of these first remote-controlled models.

Mr Revell-Control: Ten years ago, Andreas Bittlinger began to turn the RC sector of Revell Germany into a new, attractive mainstay.

When the Bünde enterprise becomes airborne in 2008 with Revell-Control, even a cockroach plays a part. Thanks to coaxial rotors, the roach as well as a beetle and a bee lift off. Andreas Bittlinger recalls: "Yes, it could take off and land. But it was virtually impossible to land it on a specific spot." In 2008, helicopters and light aircraft are also launched. Bittlinger, who very determinedly expanded the RC division in Bünde, had started his career at Adidas: "I'm very familiar with Adilette slides." Later he moves to the doll manufacturer Zapf Creation, where he experiences a real rollercoaster ride: "I lived through the meteoric rise of the brand and also the crash."

Revell had a clear-cut strategy for its RC business in Bünde: "In the beginning, of course, we bought in from outside. Later we were in a position to offer products that were a better fit to the Revell brand. And, in the RC trade, change happens quicker than with plastic kits and you can't afford to miss the technological advances. On the contrary: ideally you should be at the forefront," said Andreas Bittlinger, the RC specialist at Bünde. Indeed, in 2008, Revell made over 100,000 units of its RC program. Bittlinger continues: "We used the first years to establish ourself as an RC provider. The one important aspect for success: our spare parts service. This also set us apart from the no-name products from China." The Revell brand also enjoyed a higher level of trust in the RC field, and the team from Bünde lived

Tailored products: Revell-Control now initiates a shift in strategy. While developers initially bought in outside products, the Bünde company now has products made exclusively for them, such as the 2017-released "1080 Stunt Monster", with the stunt car line to be further expanded in 2018.

up to the expectations. "Our learning curve was fast and very, very steep," acknowledged Bittlinger.

2009 brought improved packaging with more instructions on the box. Helicopter kits included replacement rotors, since they were high-wear components. Packaging of RC products is particularly important as these technical products require explanation. The aircraft cabins were also made more appealing. Bittlinger: "Customers, of course, expected this from Revell." Moreover, the brand from Bünde released its first products that attracted a passionate fanbase: The Big One helicopter came in three different versions, with 80,000 units sold from retailers' shelves.

But by 2011, the car model came back into focus. The company came up with an advent calendar, which included mini racers with loads of accessories that could be built into a speedy racetrack. Revell's RC expert: "That was a huge success. At that time we sold 40,000 of these and turned the advent calendar into a real success story." Technical evolutions were added to the program such as Gigahertz, lipo-ion batteries and height sensors, and helicopters were fitted with electronic gyroscope systems from 2012 on, which allowed even those without fine motor skills (such as the author) to control the craft more precisely. That same year, the Moovee, Revell's first helicopter with a video camera, came on the market.

Revell can: In 2013, Revell packages its RC mini cars in a container that resembles a Cola can and thus creates the first RC million-seller in the range.

Award-winning: For its Mini Quadrocopter dubbed the Nano Quad, Revell even takes out the toy award in 2014 at the Toy Fair in Nuremberg. More awards followed.

A year later, the legendary RC mini cars were delivered in packaging reminiscent of Cola cans. These RC products sold in the millions. 1.5 million in sales put Revell at number four in the top ten. By now, Revell was no longer the new kid on the block in the RC market. "After the undisputed giant, Simba-Dickie, we are managing to crawl our way up another two positions in this area with the Carrera. And, our target group starts at six years old with no upward age limit." Now, the products are charged with a USB stick. And in 2014, Revell took home its first toy award as an RC manufacturer at the

It's all in the box: Technically sophisticated products such as the RC aircraft require comprehensive instructions on the packaging – and in several languages. Here, too, Revell-Control sets the benchmark.

Small is beautiful: Again and again, the Revell-Control brand relies on RC mini cars, which turns into a sales successes. Just how compact the modern RC cars have now become is emphasized here by this size comparison.

Interntional Toy Fair: nearly half a million of the the tiny, 12-gram Nano Quad have sold. Revell-Control has established itself in the role of the innovator.

As a consequence, Quadrocopters in various sizes, with optional cameras and sophisticated flight features, were the top sellers on the market. In 2016, RC Junior conquered very young fans in Revell-Control trim. The Revell-Control brand continued to boom, not least because the company invested in quality. Bittlinger: "When it comes to safety, we also make an effort that goes beyond the requirements of law. We take this topic very seriously. We also continually pull control articles from the current production and put them through our test lab."

In 2017, the first racer with virtual-reality glasses followed and this year Revell unveiled its first, exclusive stunt car. What now? Bittlinger explains: "Trends are changing faster and faster and they're more unpredictable. We're always on the look out for new possibilities." In any case, the numbers are on the rise. In 2017, Revell sold over 550,000 RC products, even in the higher priced segments. For 2018, Revell is planning the next RC coup and will introduce more customized stunt cars with lighting effects.

Andreas A. Berse

Bavarian story

Two classic BMW originals provide the blueprint for a pair of Revell top sellers. Behind them are two fascinating Bavarian background stories.

What does the BMW R75/5 from 1969 and the Isetta from 1955 have in common? Both are powered by a motorbike engine. But, when the Revell brand comes into play, two other stories come to light.
In 1968, young Ulli Taubert joined Revell as an apprenticel. One of his first tasks after the end of his apprenticeship in 1971 was to develop a 1:8 model of the BMW R75/5, one of the first of his own projects for Revell at Bünde. Taubert had a motorbike license and drove the black BMW R75/5 that the team at Bünde received from Munich for research purposes. He immediately fell in love with the boxer-type motorcyle and ordered himself such a bike.
August 1, 1971: Taubert took ownership of his BMW R75/5 and wanted to leave Revell to finally take up his studies. But a serious accident with his "gummikuh", the nickname given to the BMW bike amongst German motorcyclists, threw a spanner in the works. The avid biker and his pillion passenger suffered serious injuries after a VW Beetle driver veered in front of them and knocked them and the bike from the road into a ditch. The young wholesale trader spent the next six months in hospital. His University place was gone, and the BMW model from Revell was long finished. Shortly before his discharge from hospital, a small delegation visited the former Revell employee. A new export department was about to open and they needed an energetic staff member. Taubert returned to East Westphalia and stayed with the firm for five decades.
In the halls of BMW Classic, he now holds a blue BMW R75/5 in his hands, fixed with wooden sticks on a Styrofoam board. This is how such assembled models have been fixed for years so that Revell can send them to trade fairs. Another Styrofoam board is fitted on top and then it's placed in a box and sent off. Taubert: "It's a true Revell invention and simply ingenious." Incidentally, Revell plans to reissue the 1:8 kit this year. This wasn't the first time they'd

Man and machine: Ulli Taubert develops the 1:8 model of the R 75/5 for Revell, buys one himself and, due to an accident, remains with Revell Germany.

A million-seller: The 1:18-model of the Isetta is to date the best-selling finished model at Revell. Ulli Taubert suggests more than once that the management should produce it – they finally agree. Ultimately, Revell would sell over a million 1:18 Isetta kits.

A boxer's heart: The 1:8 plastic kit of the BMW R 75/5 is the first in-house development from Revell in Bünde. Its huge popularity results in many reissues over the years.

done this: "The R75/5 was a top seller from the start and it was re-released many times over the years." What about the quality in those days? "75 percent of today's quality," admits Taubert, "but it doesn't make sense to compare. There are simply new technologies today, for instance to cast much thinner plastic wheel spokes, just like on the real motorbike: Today they feature ABS which the R75/5 never had." The real life BMW motorbike painted in a special light blue livery shown here took part in the opening ceremony at the 1972 Munich Olympics.

The second story concerns the BMW Isetta. It was a meeting of the 1:1 Reseda Green original with the baby blue 1:18 version from the Revell "pre-series" of that time – a finished model with a zinc diecast body. Revell rebuilt the export version with sliding windows, whereas the original featured hinged windows and a large fabric roof. Taubert has fond memories of the bumpy road to the 1:18 model: "For four years at our conference for new items, I kept suggesting that we make the Isetta. At some point the board conceded and gave the green light for the miniaturized "pothole detector". In the words of the manager at that time: "Who wants to buy this trash?" To date, over a million customers. The lovingly created model from East Westphalia with steerable front wheels, an opening front door and removable hood is still the best-selling 1:18 product. Taubert: "I wanted to build other 1:18 models that weren't yet available on the market back then. So I came up with the idea of a small car from the economic miracle era, such as the Isetta 'canoodle ball', the Messerschmitt 'cabin scooter', aka 'people in aspic', the cute, plasticky "Leukoplastbomber" and the Lloyd Alexander, the unforgettable small car from Borgward." Although Revell had stopped producing ready-made models of

The door to success: Revell even manages to realistically recreate the opening front access door with the tilt-away steering wheel in the 1:18 Isetta.

Bike power: The one-cylinder engine powering the real Isetta is skilfully reproduced in the 1:18 model.

A hot favorite: Again and again, Revell relaunches the BMW R 75/5. And in 2018, the shapely boxer-type motorbike from Munich will boost the fleet of the model-kit makers from Bünde. And this won't be the last re-release of the boxer bike.

this scale for some years, the landmark BMW Isetta is still regarded as an unparalleld coup of Revell Germany. In the hallowed halls of BMW Classic, all four now meet – the two white-and-blue originals and the Revell "classics" in 1:8 made of plastic, as well as the 1:18 made of diecast zinc – for a rendezvous in an environment that is used for events or festive celebrations today.

The real-life Isetta proved to be a top seller from 1955 to 1962 in BMW's range and, thanks to its popularity, maneuvered the brand through difficult times. Moreover, with the Pullman Isetta type 600, the two-seater paved the way to the real car, the BMW 700. Boxer-powered bikes at BMW have been around since 1923 with the debut of the R32. The "five-series", which included the R 75/5, replaced the BMW two-wheeler with swinging fork suspension and featured a completely new design. At a top speed of 180 km/h, the R75/5 was one of the swiftest motorbikes of its time. Taubert: "When we launched our first in-house development as a 1:8 kit at Bünde, we thought, of course, that this could be a great product for Revell USA." Of course the strategists were correct in their assumption – a Bavarian success story began. One of two.

Andreas A. Berse

Trusted partner

Trust is the most important currency – and this is what Bernd Wiegmann offers his customers during his many years as sales manager at Revell.

In 1971, Bernd Wiegmann began his career as a sales promoter before working for a Revell representative in 1973. His Revell career at the headquarters in Bünde started in September 1983. Since 1976, the salesman had been solely responsible for selling model kits in the Hesse region of Germany, but now Kurt Haubrok wanted to entice him to Bünde to take on a clean-up job: to sell toys from Céji. The East Westphalian with the baritone voice recalls: "I grabbed a writing pad and we got started. The first Céji catalog had 157 products – we didn't need 154 of them." Sleuth Wiegmann established a network of excellent contacts – which proved to be a recipe for success. At the toy fair, he set up a sales team of four people, and despite his unfavorably-positioned stand at the toy fair away from the Revell stand, the Asterix figures sold like hotcakes.

Networker: Bernd Wiegmann has been associated with Revell for over 40 years, and during his time as the head of sales has earned himself a reputation that is unrivalled.

He recalls: "It was a crazy time. At the Céji headquarters in Paris, we had to give a friendly but perfunctory nod to their sales targets. The French built a huge factory for RC toys – which turned out to be a major flop." Surviving such tough times paved the way to better things. In 1986, Kurt Haubrok put Wiegmann in the next hot seat. He was to sell Revell to selected department stores. Several specialist retailers were not at all amused. Today, Haubrok explains: "We had no alternative. The sales environment was changing at that time, just like it is today with the Internet."

Four years later, Wiegmann got the job that until the end of 2015 would earn him great respect amongst experts in the toy industry: From July 1, 1987, he worked as the head of sales at Revell, and from 1989 took on the additional role of sales director, which included all export markets. "I only heard about my promotion after returning from my vacation," grins the devoted businessman.

In the turbulent seas of the toy industry's distribution system, which can at times become tempestu-

A doll for boys: Kickomania is another key to Bernd Wiegmann's success.

ous, Wiegmann always kept his head above water. "The upheavals in recent decades have been major. We once had 5,000 customers, now it's half that. There were once German department stores such as the Kaufring, DHS (Richter), Hertie and numerous wholesalers – all gone. Instead, Toys "R" Us appeared and retailers felt threatened, afraid they would sink. What's more, the Internet is rapidly changing the way we work and licensing issues are becoming more important. By contrast, conventional dispatchers like Quelle and Neckermann have disappeared."

In such stormy times, Wiegmann is regarded as a critical driving force behind a different development: In the eighties, Revell ranked second with 35 percent behind Airfix, today the Bünde enterprise sits on pole position in Germany with over 75 percent. All over Germany, Wiegmann succeeded in establishing Revell kits as an integral part of the range in every toy retail business. In Europe, Revell currently holds over 50 percent of the market share, with the runner-up at no more than eight percent.

Wiegmann also had a major say in model policy and he's not afraid to admit he sometimes got it wrong: "With the 1:18 Isetta, Ulli Taubert pestered us for four years before we relented. It turned into an absolute top seller. We all totally overestimated the popularity of the Rhine steamship Goethe as a kit. Not every shot hits the target. With the well-timed reissue of the Titanic from the original mold of the sixties in time for the movie blockbuster, we were again back up to 100,000 units. That's great fun." Sometimes Wiegmann himself got involved in model policies. When a lady at the toy fare showed him a paintbrush from Springer, which didn't roll off the table thanks to its triangular shaft, Revell didn't hesitate in giving its own painting accessories a facelift.

And the sales magician was open to new ideas. In sales, he rolled out new product lines such as die-cast, MagCliks, Grand Champions and Orbis. Football figures from Kickomania also boomed: "At first they said you can't sell dolls to boys! We then celebrated selling over a million of the product." With the change of ownership, including two management buy-outs of Revell in 2002 and 2006, Wiegmann kept his cool: "Normally when it gets too much you change jobs. At Revell in Bünde, we preferred to change the owner."

Today, the sales specialist assessment is mainly positive: "Revell has always offered quality products that the market demanded, and something even more important than that: it always had a good name." In both of these qualities, Bernd Wiegmann is not entirely without blame.

Andreas A. Berse

Department X – the secret service of Revell

Revell Germany puts a high priority on service. And hidden behind this is Department X.

Ostensibly, it's not particularly interesting to talk about the topic of 'service'. Except at Revell! It is precisely this subject that has been one of the most important since the founding of the company. It would often happen in the early days that parts would come loose from the sprues and get lost: albeit more back then than today as technology has since improved. This, of course, was a nightmare for modelers. Right from the outset, Heinz-Georg Schöneberg knew that he had to provide this spare parts service free-of-charge in order to keep modelmakers on board. Terms such as "warranty" or "product liability" didn't exist. It all started in a small room off to one side of the dispatch department on the ground floor of the old factory building in the Bünde town center. A few shelves were built by hand and a sample of each kit from the range was stored there. If we received a letter from a customer who was missing a part, our part-time "X" lady, Irmgard Feldmann, would open the appropriate kit, take out the part and send the small "product sample" to the hobbyist by mail. Even at that time, this service proved extremely time-consuming and expensive. The department added extra personnel in the months post-Christmas, as this was when modelers would assemble their Revell gifts in huge numbers and discover that parts were missing.

With the move to the new building in 1971, Department "X" expanded and was now able to fall back on two part-time staff members. Due to the higher volume, the system had to undergo changes. Today, Revell has a row of wooden cabinets with drawers, which always contain several of the pieces. The drawers are all successively numbered on the outside, and the contents of the box change every year. As soon as a missing part is ordered, the department X staff checks in which box the article is. The part is located, cut out of the sprue, placed in a small polybag, packed in a sample bag, addressed and dispatched to the customer. The average cost for handling a complaint today comes to around €7.50, which over a year represents quite a large sum, but it is certainly more effective than any TV spot or advertisement.

The question arises time and again, how long does Revell hold spare parts in stock for a product? This period of time varies between three and five years. Thus, if a customer buys an older kit at a flea market or on the market and notices that a part is missing, they can, of course, be unlucky.

"X", as it was called, was always the yardstick for retail sales. What the sales force or sales statistics could never show at the time was the actual sales outside at the toy frontline. Thus, Revell was always pleased when "X" staff members had to work overtime. This indicated that it was peak season

The customer is king: Today, if a part is missing in a current kit, buyers receive a free replacement. At Revell, the division responsible for this very special service for modelers has been dubbed "Department X".

in the retail industry rather than poorer quality products. "X" was also the outpost for eventual professional quality assurance, because as soon as a specific spare part was requested repeatedly, Revell realized that the tool needed to be adjusted. And the experts were able to do this within a short time in their own workshop linked to the production. The part would be reproduced and then sent to the modeler by "X".

An odd phenomenon within the company was the repeated attempt over the years, as suggested by some marketing manager or management director, to charge customers for this service. This very quickly failed. Revell hobbyists were now used to getting their spare parts for fre and even the attempt to charge for postage alone also failed on the market. This was definitely a reason for the popularity of Revell products and the level of awareness of this department, and thus the right decision.

In recent years, a "kit remodeling" scene has emerged, which refines or upgrades a basic kit with the help of additional parts. The required components from other Revell kits can also be ordered from "X". There, customers receive an offer on these parts and they, of course, come with an invoice. This is a service that is very much accepted and popular today.

Over the years, our "X" experts have acquired a certain degree of practice in the handling process. It is strikingly obvious in aircraft carriers, of course, that the on-board planes in the kit are often missing. The same applies to the small figures in the big sailing ships, or the rubber tires on cars and trucks. When it comes to tours of the company, anecdotes from everyday life in Department "X" are often told, for instance, how some customers try to assemble an entire kit by requesting spare parts on a weekly basis.

Ulli Taubert

Striking out for new shores

Kurt Haubrok starts his career at Revell Germany in 1963. From 1980, he takes over as managing director, initially alongside Colin Dunne from Great Britain, and later as the sole boss.

Although it's been 55 years, for Kurt Haubrok it seems like yesterday: "In 1963, a sales rep from Revell lured me to Bünde. I met the managing director at Revell Germany, Hans-Georg Schöneberg, at the Christmas party." With its products, the company had discovered a kind of "philosopher's stone". Kurt Haubrok, who stayed with Revell until 1995: "You can't imagine it today, but we distributed the products to shopkeepers. Kits were something special. They were the Gameboys of that time, a real experience."

Europe in sight: Kurt Haubrok leads Revell Germany beyond its own geographical boundaries towards the Netherlands, Belgium and onwards to East Europe.

During his career, Haubrok worked as an employee for purchasing, sales and marketing. The U.S. founder Lewis H. Glaser made a lasting impression at their first meeting: "When I saw him for the first time, the Bismarck had just been launched on the market and Glaser was bursting with new ideas. I found that exciting." Haubrok's career took off. In 1974, he was given carte blanche at Revell Germany. Two years after Hans-Georg Schöneberg left the company, the Americans gave him the role of managing director alongside Colin Dunne from the UK. Eventually he would take sole responsibility for Revell GmbH. During Haubrok's era, many decisions were made that broadened the horizon for the Bünde company. In 1974, the business expanded into the Netherlands and Belgium. Tailor-made products proved to be the key to success here. This wasn't needed in the East. Haubrok: "In the mid-seventies, we put out feelers into the Yugoslavian market. Mehano Technica was our partner there." Trade fairs in Brno, Warsaw and Prague opened the door to East Europe for the German brand. Such activities boosted Revell Germany significantly, allowing them to outpace their British contemporary. From 1980, products from Revell Germany were sold in Moscow's GUM department store.

Change of culture: Initially, kits like the Supersonic Clipper come from America, until Kurt Haubrok turns Bünde into a development center.

Haubrok was also a clever representative when it came to managing the interests of the Bünde branch compared to his American counterparts. Revell Germany printed its own cardboard boxes, assembly instructions and decals, which slashed prices and thus boosted sales. Haubrok pushed the in-house development trend, and turned Bünde from a pure sales hub to a development and production base.

In the mid-seventies, Lewis's widow, Royle Glaser, was eager to sell Revell and cash up. Kurt Haubrok has not such fond memories of this time, which almost wiped the good name from the history books. In 1979, Revell Germany was taken over by the Céji Group, a Rothschild investment company with a French toy range. On top of the oil crisis, the company had to deal with a new owner. Haubrok: "That was one of the most difficult times. The Revell name was supposed to disappear and be replaced with Céji." Moreover, Revell was forced to sell toys that were basically shelf-warmers. The search for new owners began at that moment. In 1986, the matter was in the bag: Odyssey Partners took over the Revell Group worldwide. Haubrok: "We were lucky that the Revell name hadn't disappeared."

Revell remained the cash cow of the concern, and Haubrok made the most of this. Whenever the U.S. parent ran into financial difficulties, he bought their tools. This started in 1986. Haubrok: "The injection molds are our gold, and we became increasingly more independent." At the same time, he initiated in-house productions and forged ties to Italeri, Protar, Tamiya, Lindberg and Esci. Revell Germany – Revell Ltd in England had ceased to exist – prepared itself to go public on the stock exchange in 1990, which Haubrok organized with Hans-Ulrich Remfert. Haubrok: "Initially, this whole affair was stressful for the management and not without risk. But, Revell remained on the road to success." In doing this, history helped the East Westphalians: After the Berlin wall fell, the GDR "model-building nation" joined the domestic market. Haubrok's motto: "We have always conducted intense discussions with our partners and we always fought to uphold the solution we found together. And, people are the decisive factor." For the future, the now 77-year-old hopes for one thing above all else: "If the current managing director Stefan Krings succeeds in building a third mainstay alongside kits and RC, then he's a big player."

Andreas A. Berse

Flying the flag

More than 60 years of Revell Germany are also reflected in the development of the company logo – a journey through the years.

For a start, the author takes a trip through Revell history to the early days in the USA. The first question that crops up is how Revell's name and logo came to be. I only know this story from conversations with my friend Ron Campbell, who was the technical head of Revell USA until the end of the seventies. Lew Glaser was looking for a name for his new "toy", the plastic model kit, and initiated a survey amongst the employees of his company. He showed his staff the individual parts and the finished model. It was a "Maxwell" classic car from 1913. Everyone was encouraged to make a suggestion, with Glaser's team ultimately settling on the name "Revell", for both the product and the company name. The machine operator who came up with the name received five US dollars – at least that's the story that has been handed down.

The first products in the USA at that time were called "Revell Quick Construction Kits", with the Revell name appearing only as lettering, sometimes printed in black, sometimes in red and sometimes blue. Unfortunately, no one can really recall how yellow was chosen for the name Revell with blue for the background. What is known, however, is that the red and white lines next to the logo are a salute to the American Stars & Stripes.

At the time of Revell Germany's foundation, the logo looked not a lot different to how it is today. However, it has constantly undergone change and modifications. Back then, there was no corporate identity (CI) like there is today. Hence, the graphic designers of that time would sometimes set the logo on its own, sometimes in red, or blue, or again as a flag – there were no hard and fast rules.

1957, 2004, 2016: This graphic "triple jump" of the logo shows that the kit giant was also extremely flexible with its company emblem. And the kit specialists took this to heart long before the invention of Corporate Identity. The first logo of Revell, which was founded in the United States, was still strongly influenced by the American Stars & Stripes flag.

1952 1956 1956 1965

1966 1967 1976 1979

1979 1984 1999 2004

The stripes then migrated to the left again. Hence, a colorful variation of logos appeared on the market. It was not until 1957 that the first final logo “Revell – Authentic Kits” emerged in yellow with a blue background and with red and white stripes on the right. This emblem stayed the same until 1965. In 1966, the Revell logo suddenly appeared with a black background. Revell history has shown that marketing management was usually responsible for these changes. because every time a new marketing director started in the States, the logo changed. Perhaps in keeping with the motto: a new broom sweeps clean.

The black background remained for many years – until 1978 – with the logo background changing to blue in 1979. But in this regard, too, the blue shades changed again and again over the years. And experimentation continued over the following years, especially with the catalog title. The graphic designers only used the name as a “stand alone”, sometimes in silver (1979), then in red (1980), followed by yellow (1981).

In 1982, the logo was joined by the words “the model-maker”, with this version remaining unchanged until 1984. Following this was the French era, when the Ceji Group took the helm of the Bünde company. The new owner of Revell made sure that the name Ceji was added immediately to the new version. But we survived this phase, too. At one stage, Ceji even attempted to eliminate the Revell name altogether. Through the untiring efforts of the managing director at that time, Kurt Haubrok, the original name was retained in the logo. On the contrary, the Ceji reign ended soon afterwards and the 1986 catalog once again displayed the normal Revell logo, albeit with modifications in terms of size and format.

Then began a wonderful time of diversification with new product lines receiving their own logos. In 1989, for example, there was Revell Metal or Metal Kit, Mini Dinos, Mini Jets, Advantage, Easy Kit, Pocket and much more. The actual logo, however, stayed the same, and only the product group was added. In 2004, the year in which we included slot-car racing models under the name Revell Model Racing, the slogan “Build Your Dreams” was added. Since then, the logo only supplements the Internet website www.revell.de.

Ulli Taubert

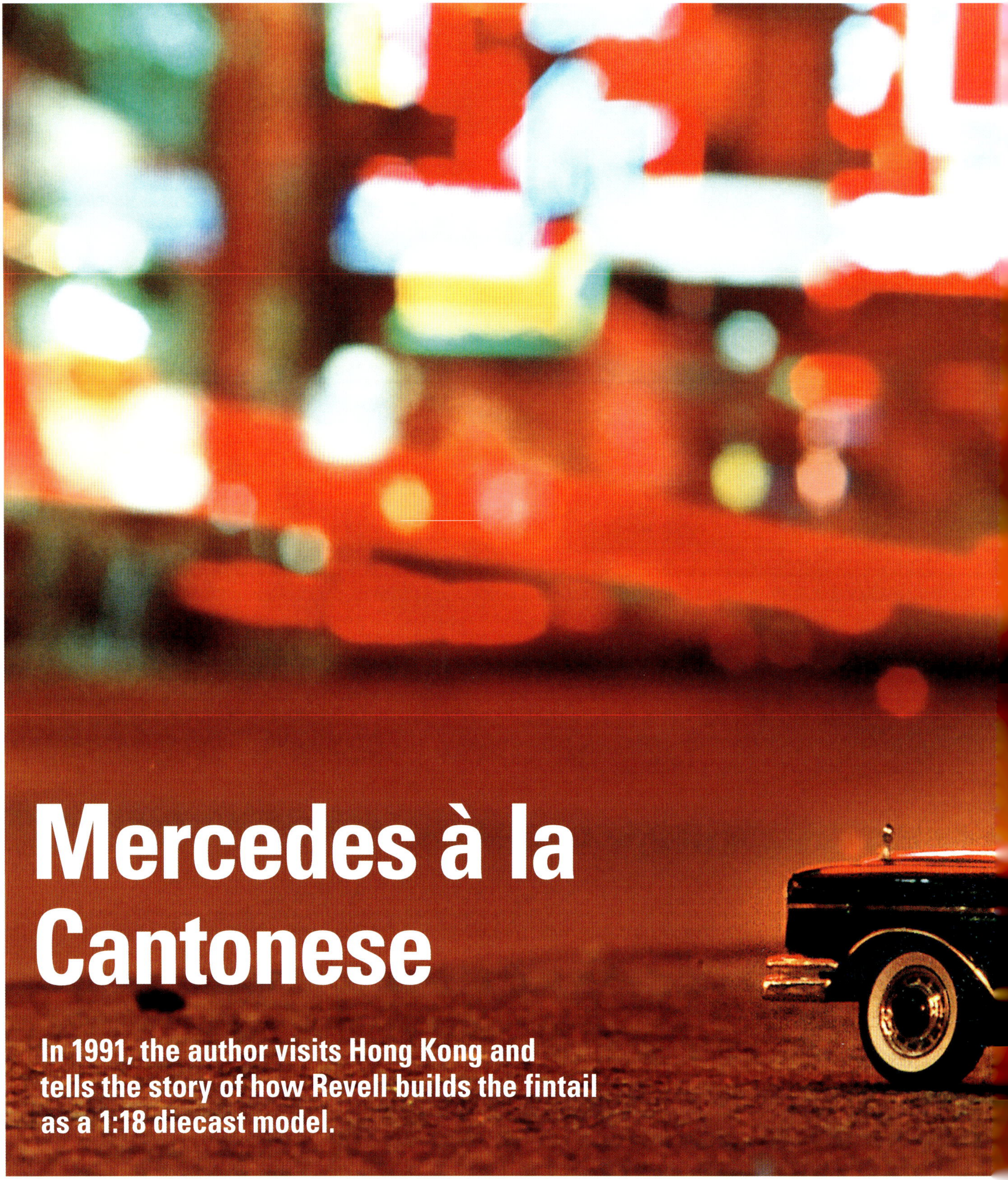

Mercedes à la Cantonese

In 1991, the author visits Hong Kong and tells the story of how Revell builds the fintail as a 1:18 diecast model.

Luxury liner: With the fintail Mercedes-Benz, Revell took the stage in the nineties building a finished model of the sedan with the star.

The Mercedes-Benz 300 SEL in 1:18, which Revell first unveiled to the public in 1995, marked a milestone – and even a revelation for collectors. Revell Germany opened a new chapter in the diecast series with the chrome-trimmed four-door car: German sedans were to become a recurring theme through the diecast fleet. The birthplace of this popular model was behind a gray facade in Hong Kong's Fui Yiu Kok Street 27 years ago. This address housed the company of S. H. Kwok, who at that time held a passport from both Britain and the People's Republic of China. Still today, it is one of Revell's most reliable partners in the field of moldmaking, production of plastic models and diecast collectors' miniatures. In 1995, Kwok stated: "German customers attach great importance on quality. When they implement a project only the best is used. You can see this with the tailfin, for example, on the chrome coating sections of the body."

At this time, moldmaking was still carried out in Hong Kong, however production of the miniatures for Revell collectors was completed behind the existing border of the British crown colony, about 50 kilometers further north in the People's Republic of China. With a day visa and thanks to the good ties of S. H. Kwok, we were also able to look around there. Sure, today, more than a quarter of a century later, Revell would certainly find different solutions to some of the details on the miniatures, but the black luxury sedan and the many sponsor logos on the racing version of the Mercedes-Benz 300 SEL added impressive highlights. Ulli Taubert: "Now we simply have new technologies, so we can do more these days with printing than was possible at that time." Two things, however, were already apparent in 1995: We aimed to achieve the best possible proportions with the miniature and strive for perfect finishes, not only in the paintwork but also in the gap dimension of the engine hood and front doors of the models and the delicate work on the interior fitout of the prestigious luxury sedan from the economic miracle era of the Federal Republic of Germany. When our team visited the production plant in the First Industrial Area in Bao, a factory in the special economic zone of Shenzhen, the place was buzzing like in a beehive. After all, model car production is predominantly manual work. Although machinery can manufacture the diecast zinc components and plastics semi-automatically, the paintwork and assembly was done by hand. With almost 100 components needing to be precisely assembled, this was no easy task. Especially when applying the chrome strips, highest precision was required. S. H. Kwok obviously put his trust in women, as they were clearly in the majority here at the assembly facilities that dealt with trims.

Global business: Already in the nineties, the production of pre-assembled diecast zinc models in the 1:18 scale is a global business. While Revell in Bünde takes the exact measurements of the corresponding originals of the classics from the Mercedes fleet and produces a dossier, the molds back then are made in Hong Kong, which was a British colony at that time. When it comes to motorbikes, sometimes the original stands in the moldmaking department (left). The assembly of the tailfin in a scale of 1:18 is carried out in the People's Republic of China.

Time is money: When the author and photographer visit the production facility of the Mercedes-Benz 300 SEL in the People's Republic of China in 1995, they encounter a hive of activity. The 35,000 tailfins in a 1:18 scale must be delivered to Germany in time for the Christmas trade.

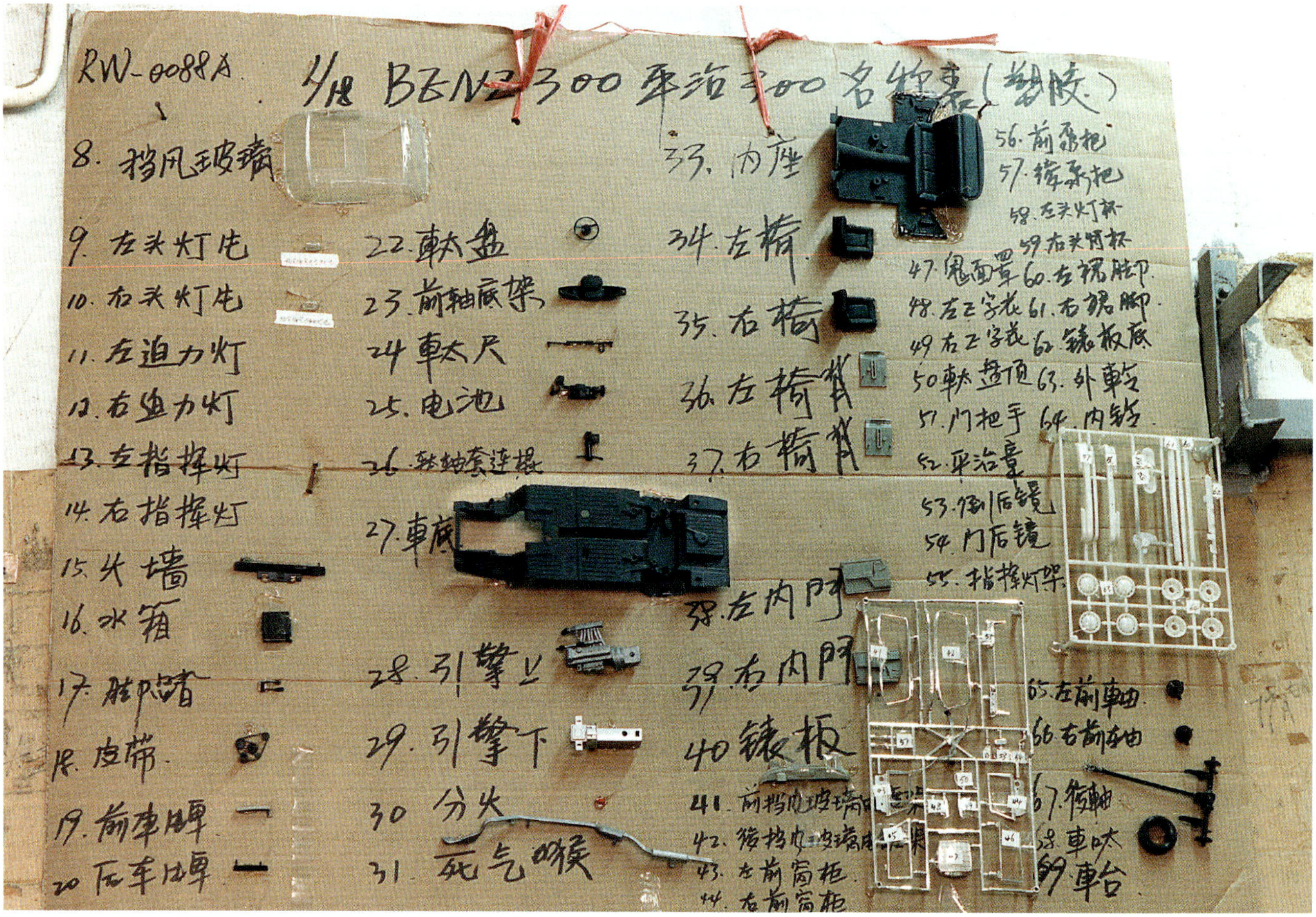

And the customers in "good old Germany" waited with bated breath. While we constantly seemed to get in the way of the bustling employees, production of the tailfin models was running at high revs for the Christmas trade. 35,000 black Mercedes-Benz 300 SEL sedans were not only to be produced, but also put into a container and transported to Germany in time to delight Revell fans when they find them under their Christmas trees. Incidentally, from this huge production run, Mercedes-Benz ordered some for its "Classic Collection" in special silver boxes, which needed very careful handling during packaging.

Car enthusiast: S. H. Kwok builds and develops the Mercedes-Benz 300 SEL for Revell and in this photo proudly holds the so-called tooling model of the novelty from Bünde, which is twice the size of the eventual miniature. BMW driver Kwok is also an automotive engineer.

At that time, the former farming village of Shenzhen was a city of 750,000 inhabitants, whereas today almost 12.5 million people live in the special economic zone 100 kilometers southeast of the provincial capital Guangzhou. But even back then, making model cars was a global business. Revell photographed and measured the originals in the Mercedes Museum, collated a portfolio for the moldmaking in Hong Kong with experts from Untertürkheim and oversaw the start of production in the People's Republic of China. To this day, nothing much has changed in the diecast business, with Revell in Bünde playing a pioneering role in this. Ulli Taubert adds somewhat wistfully: "Diecast manufacturers these days can only dream of the quantities that Revell produced back then." And this is another reason why Revell pulled out of the business years ago.

Revell sedan with the star

When Revell unveiled its first tailfin as the 300 SEL to the public in 1991, sedans in a 1:18-scale were still not really a topic. Ulli Taubert recalls: "We wanted to introduce a highlight in the diecast program. German sedans were popular. And with the 300 SEL we were also able to create the Böhringer tailfin." The background: In the early sixties, works driver Eugen Böhringer was thrashing his rally rivals at the wheel of his heavy blue sedan with a white roof, and was even crowned European vice champion in 1961.

But at Revell, the fleet of Mercedes sedans included more model series from Stuttgart. Also in the German kit-maker's range was the predecessor to the tailfin, the nicely rounded Mercedes-Benz Ponton (W120), as well as the indestructible W123 and the Mercedes-Benz 450 SEL W116 – all as zinc diecast models in 1:18.

The advantage for Revell was that the model cars with the star on the radiator proved to be popular not only amongst customers in Germany. The product planners at Revell also found other manufacturers of sedans: as was the case with the Ford 12 M and the Opel Kapitän from the sixties.

The strategist

In 1984, Hans Ulrich Remfert joins Revell as Head of Marketing and Product Development. In 1997, he is promoted to Managing Director and proves to be a successful strategist until 2016.

It all started at the toy trade fair in Nuremberg," recalls Hans Ulrich Remfert, where he met many sales colleagues at an evening event. He adds: "I immediately realized that they work hard at Revell but they also play hard." The newcomer came to the traditional model-kit company at Bünde from an international tobacco corporation. His job was to repeat what he'd done successfully for the cigarette world in the model kit industry: Marketing. Remfert: "Marketing was my world, of course, but I first had to familiarize myself with the products at Revell. The best way to do this was in product development, which still today reminds me of the small Gallic village in the Asterix comics. Successful but different."

Smart strategy: Hans Ulrich Remfert advances the internationalization of Revell significantly and successfully.

Looking back, the product developers have nothing but praise for the man who served as managing director of Revell Germany from 1997 and who gave them a long leash in their work. Ulli Taubert: "Obviously our projects had to make financial sense, this wasn't just some retreat for creatives. But, Remfert always left us to get on with our work. Plus, he gave us all the freedom we needed to develop great Revell novelties. And, strategically, I learned more from Hans Ulrich Remfert than I did from anyone else."

As an entrepreneur, important decisions were made during his era. In 1990, Revell AG went public, in 1994 Binney & Smith took over in East Westphalia, in 1995 the marketing expert integrated the coloring pencil brands Crayola and Revell Airbrush into the product range. With Alpha International in 2001, the Revell Group LLC in 2002, the International Group LLC in 2006, the latter two with him as co-shareholder, and Hobbico in 2012, the manager used his considerable negotiating skills to maneuver the company through four changes of ownership – each time without a fuss and, more importantly, in a way that the company could always continue successfully without any interruptions. In this way, the amenable man, who now enjoys traveling the world, left no doubt

Model policy: With regard to model policy, Revell puts a great deal of trust in Remfert. Thus, concepts such as the BMW Nazca in 1:24 and 1:18 come to fruition.

that his loyalty always lay with the Bünde company. Over the course of his career, Remfert turned into a true-blue "Revellist". A transformation that is mirrored in many employees and executives who have worked at this fascinating company in East Westphalia. The staff turnover at Henschelstrasse 20-30 is as low as the team spirit is high.

Remfert briefly describes his personal strategic approach for Revell Germany: "Internationalization with inhouse companies or distribution partners, product diversification, courage to innovate in the core business!" The question of what Revell gave him in return catches the active pensioner a little offguard. Hesitating for a moment, he gives an interesting answer: "I was simply a cog in the big wheel at the two giant corporations prior to Revell. At Revell I was lucky enough to take responsibility for the big picture for many years. Not to mention that the many and varied international activities, both in purchasing and production as well as in sales, added extra spice to my job. Above all, I feel a great deal of satisfaction and, to this day, an unwavering connection to the company."

In February 2016, Remfert handed the reins to Stefan Krings. It is part of the company's philosophy that this would herald a new era that will shape the company for decades to come. When a journalist asks Remfert if he became tougher as a manager over time, he immediately answers: "Towards the respective owners of Revell, yes, to my own team, not at all. And believe me, there is nothing tougher than having to dismiss someone in the interests of the company, these were the most wrenching times." Hans Ulrich Remfert adds one last thought: "I'm a firm believer in medium-sized companies, their power and willingness to take calculable risks. They are the hidden champions and Revell is one of them." And Remfert undoubtedly played a major role in this.

Andreas A. Berse

No brick in the wall

Early on, right after the fall of the Berlin wall, Revell becomes interested in the Trabant, the East German people's car – an unprecedented success story.

In the early eighties at the start of the model car boom, Ulli Taubert in his role as car-kit developer suggested on several occasions to follow up the model of the most famous car in the West, the VW Beetle, with the most famous car of the East, the Sachsenring Trabant. For years, his proposal fell on deaf ears ... until September 11, 1989. With the opening of the border between Austria and Hungary, hundreds and then thousands of "Trabis" poured into Germany – the wall was penetrable!

Swift "racing cardboard": The Trabant underlines how fast the Revell team at Bünde can develop something from scratch. The first 1:24 kit of the cult vehicle from the former GDR is created within just four months.

In October 1989, Taubert finally got the green light to develop a Trabi in 1:24, but not in time for the 1991 trade fair, no, the model had to be finished in 1990. This gave his team just four months instead of the usual twelve to pull it off. "I quickly got hold of an original Trabant from the Nuremberg "reception camp" without paying any attention to the quality, model year and original condition. It was a 601 S DeLuxe, recognizable by the two-tone color. I then rolled this original onto the back of a truck and transported it to the toolmakers in Denmark, where it was measured and photographed using primitive means by today's standards. Afterwards, Revell compiled the specifications with as few parts as possible. This meant no engine, no moving hoods or doors, plastic tires instead of rubber, cast with the rims in one piece – it was almost as austerely equipped as the original. We would have had to produce the rubber tires in Japan and that would have taken too long. In the end the kit was made up of only 60 individual pieces. Despite the tight timeframe and the improvised approach, the final product was perfectly dimensioned and a precise fit. The model appeared on the shelves of retailers just in time for the Nuremberg Toy Fair of 1990. Over the following years, this model turned into the most successful car kit Revell ever made.

Shortly after we launched this kit on the market, Eckard Reipke from Oerlinghausen approached us. He had acquired the last two-stroke Trabant to

The Trabi range: The first Trabant kit in 1:24 from 1990 is followed by a redesigned version based on CAD data. Five years later, the East Westphalians throw themselves into the hatchback Universal. Moreover, the limited editions that were produced have become sought-after rareties today.

roll off the assembly line and wanted to present it in a special livery to the then Federal Chancellor Helmut Kohl on the occasion of a garden party in Bonn, which he then did. Reipke wanted to have a special edition of 911 (!) units of this Trabi in its own packaging with a copy of the original certificate airbrushed on the engine hood. No sooner said than done. He then sold these 911 kits at a price of 100 Deutschmarks each and co-financed a new kindergarten in Bad Salzungen with the proceeds. It goes without saying that this kit is now a much sought-after rarity.

In January 1991, the movie Go Trabi Go was released in theatres and became a big hit. Parallel to the release of this film, Revell put out a special edition of the Trabi with the movie poster as the title. Even today we enjoy close ties to the actor Wolfgang Stumph (who played Udo Struutz in the movie). He actually has all the Revell Trabis ever released as part of his collection. By popular request, we launched a racing version of the works-run Trabi in 1995. Note: like the original the vehicle itself wasn't modified. After only 1,500 kits had been delivered, Revell received a temporary injunction from the public prosecutor's office. What had happened?

A mother had complained about the model, because the names of the drivers were included in the decal and one driver had a German surname that was deemed inappropriate for children, which in this case meant we had to stop production. For this reason and the fact that we only produced a very small number, this kit has significant value today among collectors. In 2009, 20 years after the fall of the Berlin wall, Revell decided to create a completely new but this time modern, high quality Trabi kit – but now with plenty of time for the development. For this, my Trabant specialists Detlef Rotha and Helmut Rebs spent a great deal of time researching to find a truly original 601 S.

The development department then scanned a photo of the car, which provided the database with absolutely consistent measurements as the foundation for the model. The entire project was created using CAD. In contrast to the first Trabi, the aim was to launch a model in Tamiya quality, which we succeeded in doing. As a reissue, the new Trabi had 140 individual parts, with a movable engine hood and trunk lid, however to maintain its structural integrity, the doors were not movable. Rubber tires were non-negotiable as was the detailed engine and perfect interior and chassis. On the occasion of the "Modell Hobby Spiel" in Leipzig, we got hold of an original that same year and had the design done by the Leipzig Graffiti Community during the fair. The theme was supplied to the graffiti artists, namely the 20th anniversary of the fall of the Berlin wall. Afterwards, Revell auctioned the original on the Internet and the proceeds went to the German Childhood Cancer Aid. Of course, this "Mauerfall-Trabi I" was produced as a limited edition with 1,989 kits. 2.50 Euros of each sold kit went to the charity.

Five years later, the next episode of the Trabi story unfolded. Revell decided to bring out a hatchback version of the Trabi on the occasion of the 25th anniversary of the Berlin wall coming down. In this case, too, we relied on our Trabi expert Detlef Rotha to do the research and preliminary work. With about 50 percent of the parts having to be newly developed, this job proved to be relatively straightforward.

Like we did five years earlier, for this project, we again acquired and restored an original Universal from our Trabi guru Bert Oehlgart from Bad Köstritz. The newly registered car was again spraypainted and decorated by the Leipzig Graffiti team on the occasion of the 2014 "Modell Hobby Spiel" in Leipzig, the theme this time was the 25th anniversary of the fall of the Berlin wall. Revell again auctioned the original to the highest bidder in favor of the Childhood Cancer Aid. Incidentally, both of these "Mauerfall" Trabis are still road-legal today and can be seen out and about in everyday traffic.

Recently, in 2017, Revell launched another limited edition on the 60th anniversary of the Trabant – but as a gift set with paints and crafting materials. Revell's Trabi Story has come to an end ... for the time being. There are still some versions and variants, which have already been researched, for instance the cabriolet and the Kübel. Let's wait and see when these come to fruition.

Ulli Taubert

Perfect in every detail: While the first Trabant from 1989 has imperfections in the finer points due to the short development time, the second Trabant version features many outstanding details, as shown here with the hatchback Universal in a scale of 1:24.

The Angels of the Seas

The teamwork between the German Maritime Search and Rescue Service and Revell is a real success story.

In 1985, the German Maritime Search and Rescue Service (DGzRS) introduced a new standard class, the so-called "27.5-meter" class. Revell immediately zeroed in on these ultra-modern search and rescue boats. Already at that time, and especially thanks to Revell's great ties to the Danish company Heljan, the product planners aimed to focus more and more on civilian themes in the shipping sector. Launched up until now was the research vessel Meteor, the dredger Geopotes, the Rhine paddle steamer Goethe, and the Baltic Sea ferry Finnjet – all with great success. However, 70 percent of the civilian ship kits were sold in Germany, thus the focus was put on national models.

And so, we shone the spotlight on the search and rescue theme. The development team made contact with the operator, in this case the headquarters of

A matter of the heart: Search and rescue ships like the Hermann Marwede not only belong to the top sellers in the Revell range, but are also something very dear to Revell's heart. A portion of the proceeds go to the tireless rescue teams who work along the German coast.

the German Maritime Search and Rescue Service in Bremen. From day one of this cooperation, Revell would talk directly to the managing director Dr Bernd Anders and the PR manager Andreas Lubkowitz. Both of these gentlemen were delighted with the idea and supported the projects superbly. In 1987, Revell made headway with the development of the Berlin. This ship was anchored in Laboe, hence that's where we began our research. Although all ships were categorized in the 27.5-meter class, the six boats in this category differed significantly from each other. For instance, the ships that plied the Baltic Sea region were equipped with square portholes, whereas the boats in the North Sea had oval portholds. Revell, however, only launched kits in the Baltic Sea variant. Over the years, we named our model the Berlin (from 1988 to 1993 and 2013 to 2018), or the Arkona (2000 to 2009).

One major leap in the expansion of our joint venture was the development in 2005 of the world's largest rescue ship, the Hermann Marwede stationed on Helgoland. This original model was created as a huge kit in the collector scale of 1:72 (available 2005-2008 and 2015-2017). In this case, too, we received incredible support from the DGzRS, starting with the photo shoot through to the official model launch with a press conference on board the ship. The rescue crew

Press conference at sea: The Hermann Marwede crew at the presentation of the Revell model kit. The press conference takes place in proper style on board the state-of-the-art SAR boat.

helped with PR actions and also treated the entire Revell development team to a "special crossing" from Cuxhaven to Helgoland.

Over the course of this partnership, the scaled-down "beginner's version" was launched in a scale of 1:200 (2011-2017) as well as the first smaller SAR boat of the Marwede, which was originally called Verena but now sails under the name of Walter Rose (2014-2015), followed by the rigid hull inflatable, also christened the Verena (from 2018).
All of our contacts have now gone into retirement. But even today, Revell continues to receive exemplary support from the successor Christian Stipeldey and his crew. We still have close ties to the old guard from the Hermann Helms (Jörg Bünting), the Berlin (Michael Müller), the Anneliese Kramer (Holger Wolpers) and the Hermann Marwede (Jörg Rabe). Over all the years, Revell has also supported the work of the DGzRS with its kits and given something back. Initially, a fixed amount per kit went to the Maritime Service team, later Revell gave an annual donation to Bremen based on a fair fixed license agreement. This extremely successful cooperation will continue in the future and will definitely be expanded.

Ulli Taubert

The scale of all things: Revell produces its plastic kits of the SAR ships in the scales of 1:72 and 1:200 (see photo). So far, the Berlin, the Arkona and the Hermann Marwede served as exemplary role models, including authentically reproduced rescue boats with names such as Verena.

Revell's one-of-a-kind

For decades now, Thomas Effnert has fulfilled an important role at Revell: his job is to create showpieces of novelties that don't yet exist.

Thomas Effnert is the man who creates things that will only make their debut a few months down the track. Since 1990, the trained carpenter has built very specific models. They are on display in glass cabinets, on which visitors to trade fairs press their noses: they are prototypes of upcoming creations that will only materalize in the future. His first prototype was the Ferrari Mythos in 1990.

Thomas Effnert: Earlier he created handmade samples, today he customizes parts using a stereolithography process and turns them into real highlights for Revell display cabinets at trade fairs all over the globe.

Effnert joined Revell in 1981 with his father Peter. The German model-kit maker had advertised for a modeler to build exhibition pieces. Effnert: "I was discovered by Volker Vahle, and Ulli Taubert turned me into a master modelmaker." In 1985, Taubert approached Effnert and asked: "Could you convert a conventional Mercedes 190 and a Ford XR3i into Kamei tuning versions from which we can derive the kits." Today Effnert admits: "At first I had no idea whatsoever how to do this."

Eventually over the course of his unusual career, he adapted the technique of rib construction from ship models and applied it to his prototypes, for example the Isetta in 1:18. Effnert: "Small parts and wheels could rarely be taken from the well-stocked 'spare parts box'. More often than not, the rims, for instance, would have to be made from scratch using a lathe or a so-called rotary table." The most complex model from this era at Revell never actually came on the market: The Porsche Boxster in 1:18.

Modern technology, however, is making this task increasingly easier. The avid motorcyclist: "In the times of CAD design, Revell can have the scaled body forms of future projects made using the so-called stereolithography process (STL)." For this, a 3D body shape is created out of laser-cured plastic. Effnert: "This process completely changed the way I worked. Now we have at least one precise body surface of the Revell product to use as a starting platform." However,

Handcrafted works of art: When Thomas Effnert begins his career at Revell as a prototype specialist, CAD data doesn't yet exist. Hence, the trade fair designs, such as the BMW Isetta as a 1:18 miniature, are created using a very special form of rib construction, which the expert then perfects.

the passionate judoka remarks: "An STL pattern is not just any STL pattern. Today, Revell sources the best from Italy." Instead of spending 150 hours inventing a model from scratch, this time is halved thanks to cutting-edge technologies.

Effnert, however, does much more for Revell. With the help of a small team of handpicked suppliers, he also builds most of the exhibition samples of the conventional kits, which Revell displays at trade fairs. When the first samples, also known as First Shots, arrive in his workshop, the virtuoso throws himself into the task. At the same time, he produces many images for the packaging and also adds his input to the decal design. The motor racing enthusiast: "I'm firmly convinced that my decades of experience and modern technology continue to help me in this." And sometimes he offers important insights into how the products can be improved. The 59-year-old: "But the best thing about my job was when I got to meet my motorsport heroes, such as the motorcycle world champion Giacomo Agostini, the five-time Le Mans winner Frank Biela, two-time WRC champion Walter Röhrl and Le Mans winner Hans Herrmann. Now that's great cinema."

Andreas A. Berse

Plastic that dream cars are made of

In an ultra-modern high-tech facility in Poland, Revell produces and packages plastic kits such as the Mercedes-AMG SLS in 2011 – a glimpse behind the scenes.

Revell is one of Europe's most prestigious brands in the toy and leisure field. Let's look at the numbers: In Germany, Revell with its 136 employees holds a market share of around 80 percent in the field of plastic kits. This slice of the pie is possbily matched by Maggi seasonings, but certainly not by the CSU political party in Bavaria. Believe it or not, in 2011 alone, when this report was compiled, the company from Bünde produced as many as 3.3 million kits.

Gullwing doors: The components of Revell kits, as shown here on the Mercedes-AMG SLS in 1:24, are created by a company in Poland from plastic using a so-called injection molding process.

Here's another even more impressive figure: Every year, Revell sells over 400,000 plastic car kits, from low-slung sports cars to huge American trucks. In the year 2010, as an example, the Bünde brand sold 30,000 kits of the Mercedes-AMG SLS as the gullwing coupé to hobbyists. And there is still plenty of demand for these 1:24 plastic kits.

To satisfy such demands, the injection molding machines at the Polish factory at 113 Hutricza Street in Bydgoszcz are running hot, these days predominantly due to the coupé with 571 hp under the hood. It is here that the plastic kits with no less than 141 high-precision parts are made. With movable gullwing doors and engine hood as well as an authentically reproduced V8 AMG engine in the nose, these kits inspire collectors all over the world. Incidentally, the material from which children's dreams are made is standard commercial polystyrene, which is injected into steel molds. The lurid green Engel injection molding machines are some of the best money can buy, costing up to 250,000 Euro. Seven of these machines run at full revs in the production facilility of KA Plast.

But machines alone don't make good components for a plastic kit. Nobody knows this better than Revell production manager Holger Eidberger. "Take AMG's SLS as an example. It's all about the fine-tuning. You need to keep an eye on the temperature of the plastic as its being injected. The reseating pressure has

Precision work: The injection molding machines that make high-precision plastic parts are introduced after the Second World War. In the early fifties, Revell founder Lewis Glaser invests in this new technology to make model dreams come true.

to be just right, and the cooling should be perfectly adjusted to the kit parts." If this sounds like a secret recipe, it's because it is. During the injecting process, the temperature of the plastic can fluctuate between 220 and 235 degrees Celsius (428-455 degrees Fahrenheit). The plastic itself consists of tiny granules, which pass directly from a container one floor above the production technology from preheated tanks into the injecting machine. This, too, involves high-tech. Everything is controlled by computers. Przemyslaw Dezakowski from the marketing department at the company KA-Plast in Bydgoszcz: "Laypeople may at first think that a part simply drops out of the mold, so what's the big deal? But it's definitely not as straighforward as that."

Ultimately, 2,500 new plastic kits of the Mercedes-Benz SLS AMG have to be ready for dispatch by the following afternoon, completely packaged with assembly instructions, decal sheets, tires and all other components. The managing director of KA Plast, Grzegorz Kapka: "We offer a comprehensive service here, right through to loading the finished plastic kits on to the trucks ready to hit the shelves of retailers." Other international suppliers also come into play here. The SLS as a 1:24-scale plastic kit has long been an international business. The steel molds into which the parts of the super sports car with the star are injected come from China. To develop miniatures is almost as expensive for Revell in Bünde as it is to develop a real SLS: The cost of developing such a product, including all research and moldmaking with multiple design correction stages from Mercedes-Benz itself, comes to about 120,000 Euro. The real Mercedes-Benz SLS AMG as a coupé is available for just over 180,000 Euro.

As if controlled by magic, the two parts of the finely polished steel mold are joined together. Invisible from the outside, the gray granules are then injected inside. After 38 seconds, arguably the most characteristic part of Revell's plastic kit falls out of the machine; the body of the sporty coupé. Katarzyna, the employee standing next to this production machine, inspects each and every sample, checking the gloss of the body surface under a special lamp, then trimming the sprue that protrudes from the rear window of the body part. Only then is the bodyshell put into a box for eventual packaging.

Spotless work: Before experts clamp the hardened steel molds together, they are very carefully checked and cleaned.

Strong duo: In order to form a sprue for a Revell kit, an upper and lower steel mold is required.

Crowning point: The upper mold section can be clearly seen here, from which the body of the 1:24 Mercedes-AMG is made.

The Mercedes body is born: After the injection, the mold is opened and the body automatically falls out.

The steel treasure: For the molds of a plastic kit, Revell often invests a Euro sum in the five-digit range.

Revell's profile: The molds for tires are no easy process, either. Here it is important that the tread looks as authentic as possible.

Grzegorz Kapka: "We manufacture the plastic parts from such modern steel molds with an accuracy of less than a few hundredths of a millimeter. When polishing the outer surface, we're working in the micro-range, we're talking about thousandths of a millimeter."

The smaller SLS components in a Revell kit are fixed on a large sprue, a type of plastic frame to which all the parts are attached. Hobbyists can easily paint the tiny parts such as the mirrors, gear-shift levers and seats, before detaching them from the sprue and assembling them. In this regard, the devil is in the details. Are the mounting points correct so that the components fit together perfectly? And are the suspensions for the movable gullwing doors of the Mercedes-Benz SLS AMG in 1:24 delicate enough to look as authentic as possible yet robust enough to hold the doors in place? Even in the construction, there are many conflicts of interest to solve.

Chrome rims, filigree chassis parts, the components for the interior and the tailor-made body – all of these modules are now produced and nimble fingers ensure that they are packaged together with the assembly instructions and decals into a transparent bag, and placed into the appropriate Revell box. In its debut year, the plastic kit with 141 parts cost 19.90 Euro. A perfectly assembled model measures exactly 193 millimeters. And, like the original, it represents skilful lightweight construction. The finished SLS in 1:24 tips the scales at just 151 grams.

Andreas A. Berse

Ready for battle: Anakin's Jedi Starfighter (left) and the X-Wing Fighter are just two of the stars from the Star Wars Empire at Revell.

Model you must!

May the kit be with you: Bünde in East Westphalia becomes the home of the Jedi Knights of the Star Wars kits in 2005.

The research began in 2004, that's 27 years after the first Star Wars movie hit the big screens and teleported cinema into a new era. Jürgen Zurnieden, guardian of the Star Wars project at Revell: "Revell has always offered science fiction models, but this heralded a whole new era. In time for the release of Episode III, *The Revenge of the Sith*, in 2005, Revell at Bünde added the first products to its portfolio. Zurnieden: "That was a huge leap into the movie world, whether with Lucasfilm at Skywalker Ranch or the colleagues at Disney from 2012. The huge collections of film exhibits were impressive, including the one at the new location in San Francisco with the 1:1 Yoda statue made of resin.

Over the years, Revell created a wide range of Star Wars fighters, not only developing simple, pre-painted kits – some even with figurines – under the slogan "Build and Play", but also larger models, which ambitious modelers could then fine-tune. Zurnieden: "The production run of some products over the years reached well into the six-digit range. We also supplied the international markets." The research for the X-Wing-Fighter and Co. was not always easy: After all, most of the originals existed only as animations. The Star Wars guru from Bünde adds: "We received photos of the models, which were also used for trick shots. Some of them were incredibly detailed in the cockpit area. Plus, as is commonplace with all the other projects now, the CAD data we received was very comprehensive." Especially in the Internet era, secrecy is a major problem. It goes without saying that no details should be leaked before the release of a new movie from the Star Wars series. One weak link in the chain could be disastrous. Zurnieden: "For this reason I sometimes have to announce five new products for the latest movie and show five nice

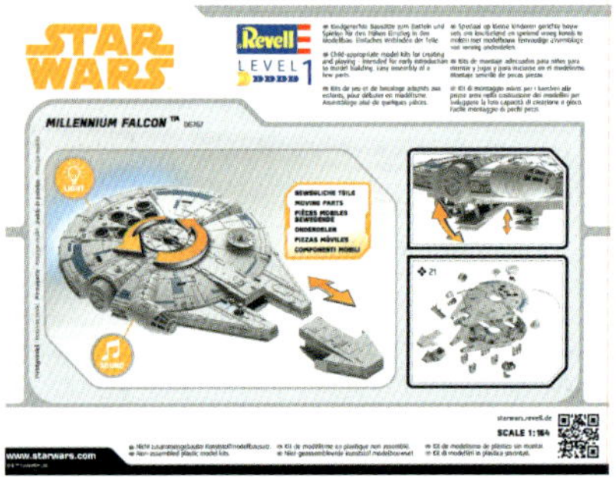

Kits to go with the movie: The Millennium Falcon in its latest version from 2018 (top) and the Heavy Assault Walker with light effects (right) for the large cannon.

Star Wars veteran: For over 40 years now, the Millennium Falcon flies through the galaxies fighting for freedom, mostly with Chewbacca and Han Solo as the pilots. In Revell's cosmos, the somewhat unusual spaceship is another star in the sci-fi range.

images of an empty universe." And how is it working with marketing people in the film industry? Jürgen Zurnieden fires back an answer faster than Yoda can draw a sword: "Whether it's Lucasfilm or Disney, the development is surprisingly structured and Revell also enjoys a high level of trust there. We've earned ourselves a good reputation over the years. As an example, perhaps our ideas with packaging are somewhat more precise than with other licensed products. They know exactly what they want."

Of course, the Star Wars universe also has its legendary spaceships. Zurnieden: "At Revell, we've been dealing with so-called A-products, which are central to the movie. The Millennium Falcon has gained cult status." If the spaceship of Star Wars hero Han Solo was a car, would it now fly with a special license plate as a craft of historic value? Other top sellers are the X-Wing Fighter and the T-Fighter, which have sold extraordinarily well in very different scales and finishes.

Above all, however, the Star Wars theme has a strategic function for Revell. The series from Revell Germany taps into the young market and brings tomorrow's modelers into the fold. That's why Revell is keen to continue nurturing this product range in the future, as well. May the force be with them! Or, as Chewbacca would say: "Rawrgwawggr!"

Andreas A. Berse

Revell's Italian dressing

Developing models requires international cooperation, especially today. Mario Falconi from Rome is an extremely important specialist for Revell in this field.

Mario Falconi, born in Rome in 1939, started his career at Monogram Models in Chicago in 1968, the same year I joined Revell in Germany. He began as a model designer in the design department there, today his job title would be engineering draftsman. But before switching to technical product development, he worked his way through several departments. For example, the Model Shop, where he was involved in developing master models, patterns and castings – in other words, all major steps from the concept to toolmaking. His first project was the original wooden model for the Monogram Saturn V in 1:144. Afterwards he was promoted to second-in-command of design, where he was also responsible for assisting projects in the model and tool shop. This is where his dream turned to reality. Mario had the perfect job, because now he could do what he'd always wanted.

The expert: With Mario Falconi, Revell lures a specialist for model development in 1987, who enhances product quality and introduces new materials.

In 1987, he decided to move back to Rome. Before doing this, however, he had a discussion with his boss, Jim Foster, who introduced him to the Revell boss at that time, Kurt Haubrok from Bünde. Haubrok set up a telephone call with Mario and attempted to lure him to our product development team as a freelancer. He accepted. Mario immediately leapt aboard our Revell team and launched himself into the next stage of his modelmaking life. Some background information: To this day, Revell's product development department at Bünde is made up of business people rather than engineers – and almost all of them have gotten where they are on their own. An expert like Mario Falconi was, of course, a wonderful addition to the team. Now, he could teach Revell a whole raft of technical things that could be of use to us in the future. From day one, Mario got involved in many projects, his forte was automobiles, where he was given responsibility for the kits as well as the ready-made diecast models for sketches, the layout of parts, blown-up drawings and mold layouts. Over the years and particularly at the annual tours around

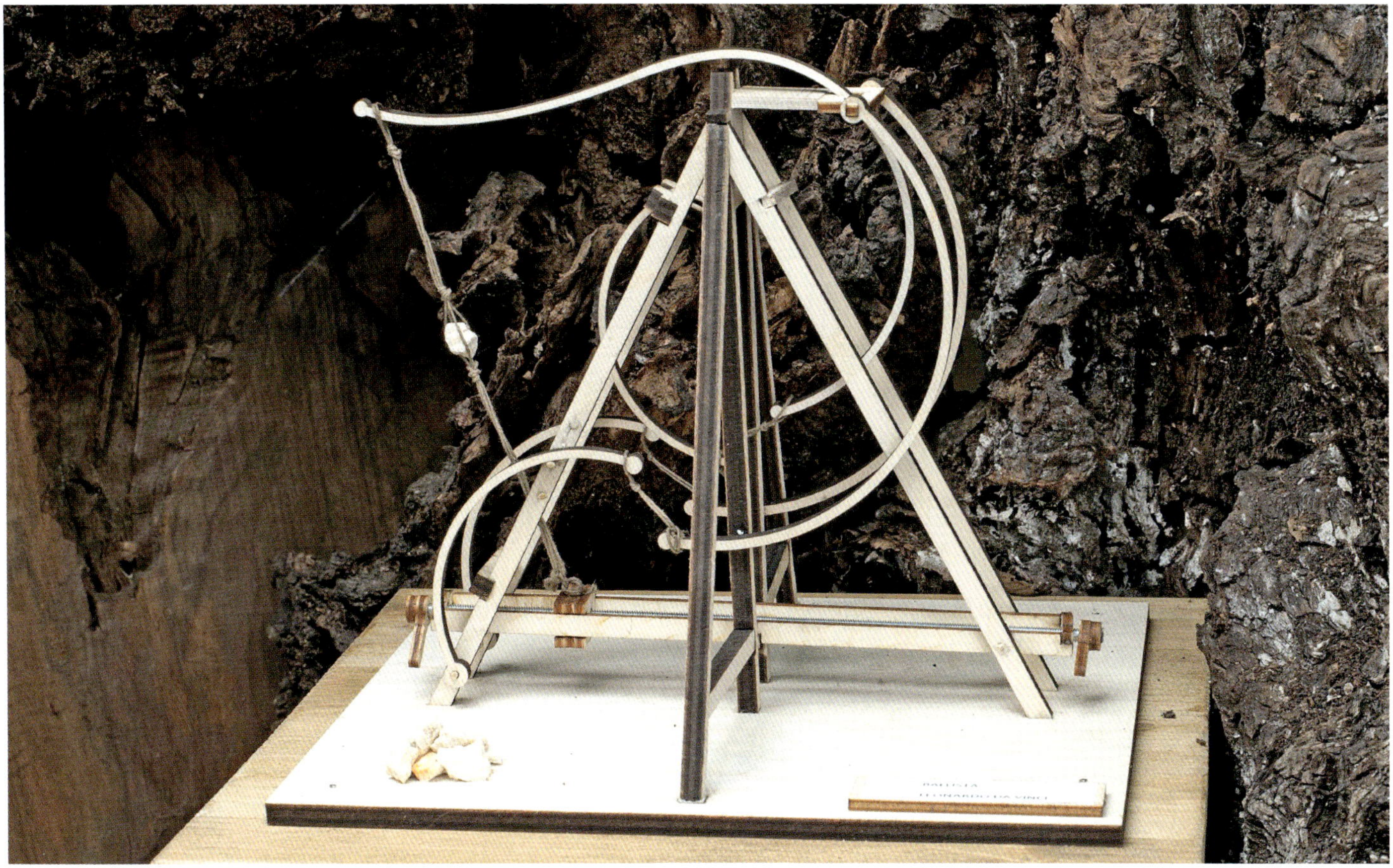

Revell's stroke of genius: When Revell's product planners come up with the idea of scaling down Leonardo da Vinci's inventions into kits, Mario Falconi facilitates the creation of the new products from laser-cut wood. Today, these kits have achieved an unparalleled cult status amongst Revell fans.

Italy, he established excellent personal ties to Italian manufacturers such as Ferrari, Maserati, Bugatti, Lamborghini as well as designers like Giugiaro and Pininfarina. Moreover, he was close to our Bologna partners, Italeri and Protar, where he could virtually come and go as he pleased. Now approaching retirement age, Mario is still a workaholic, always on the go and constantly coming up with new ideas. He has even created inventions and the corresponding prototype models. Whenever Revell came up with a new idea, the developers would immediately get Mario on board. And, thanks to Mario Falconi, this is also how a project that was initially thought of as a warm-up exercise was turned into reality and ended up in the hands of customers: Leonardo Da Vinci's inventions as kits with laser-cut parts made of wood. From the start, Mario Falconi took control as project manager and got in touch with the Milan Museum for Art and History, with whom Revell had an exclusive contract. Two-dimensional construction, assembly instructions, original models and the building of prototypes were some of his responsibilities. The "Leonardo" series began in 2010 and was temporarily stopped in 2014. A reissue and expansion of this line is very likely, but with a new overall concept. Mario Falconi is still active today, although not with quite the intensity of the past. But he is certainly an important member of the big Revell family.

Ulli Taubert

On the lookout

Stefan Krings has been managing director of Revell GmbH in Bünde since January 2016 and has already navigated the company through a change of ownership smoothly and efficiently.

January 2016 ushered in a change of guard at management level for Revell GmbH. Hans Ulrich Remfert, who had been with Revell since 1984, stepped down and handed the baton to Stefan Krings. The newcomer had previously worked as managing director for the German-speaking markets at the Italian toy manufacturer Giochi Preziosi, and prior to that was signed on with the video game giants THQ and Nintendo of Europe.

Car buff: Stefan Krings got to know and love cars from his father's car repair workshop. That and his other experiences would lend him inspiration for new products.

For Rhinelanders, there is not a lot of difference between the gamer and model-maker target groups. "Both are very dedicated to their hobbies, both like to delve deep into learning and both love spectacular things." Krings is definitely no job-hopper. And, thanks to his background, he has a great deal of experience in the licensing business. After only two years on the job, the 49-year-old has been faced with a delicate task, the same one that all of his predecessors have come up against several times and have handled with great skill. To find a new owner for Revell that can open up new prospects for the German company. With the international Munich-based investment group Quantum Capital Partners (QCP), he seems to have achieved this.

During the toy fair, while the search for a new owner was still underway, Krings told the author: "Revell is strong and that's why we're looking for an owner that fits in with us." Typical of the new managing director: confident without being arrogant and always with his sights firmly set on the brand's traditions. This, however, doesn't rule out new ideas or additional mainstays. In this respect, QCP gives Krings even more options. In the future, stronger strategies will emerge from Bünde than from the United States. And, the U.S. brand must first set up a completely new sales network. The implications coming from retailers in the United States: There would be no model construction without Revell. It's a strong statement, but with 50% of the market share it's not surprising.

A small, red tractor: The Porsche Junior 1:24-scale kit is an undisputed technological showpiece at Revell. This plastic kit paves the way for the Easy Click series, with which the Bünde bunch is eager to lure novice modelers. This could give an immense boost to brand's target market in the future.

Hans Ulrich Remfert, who played a decisive role in the selection of the new head, says: "At Revell the chemistry of the new managing director must dovetail with the company culture. And that's precisely why Stefan Krings is the right person." The newcomer also dares to look beyond the horizon: "If we can become even more efficient, that gives us a wider range of options for new projects, which in turn will guarantee a high-quality product range for us." Indeed, Krings' upbringing qualified him for this job: His father ran an independent car repair workshop that focused on Mercedes vehicles. The fact that Krings Jr has gasoline in his blood is underlined by what he does as a hobby: exploring American highways on a Harley-Davidson. And Krings knows how to strategize: Had Revell not given up the Hobbico market long ago, the difficulties of the former owner would have thrown the East Westphalian company into hot water. This decision has proven to be the right one.

Krings main focus is to expand the potential customer base. To this effect, new and successful product lines are introduced in the Junior Kit range for very young hobbyists as well as Easy Click. The latter kits can be assembled and enjoyed by all ages. Hence, the target group is huge. Krings: "Easy Click plastic kits have become everyone's darling. And, assembling them has turned into a great experience for the mainstream." The avid biker tackles the challenge with confidence: "We are the largest supplier in an extremely well-functioning market. So it's up to us to expand and control this field."

Krings, however, by no means neglects the accessories range: "This segment is very important, because it earns us steady revenue. Here too we'll step up our efforts to create new products for our customers. These are consumer products. Paints and accessories will turn into a product category in its own right." After all, paints are purchased by customers who have never before built a plastic kit. In fact, Revell at Bünde will soon launch an adhesive that hardens only under UV light. Krings: "This can be used not only for plastic kits but for other things as well."

In the future, Krings is eager to combine special products in the RC (radio-controlled) field and Junior Kits. "This is in the initial stages but it'll definitely happen in the medium term." Foil for the color design of model kit bodies could also be a new highlight. Also on the drawing board: Touring trucks from famous musicians."

Finally, Krings follows up with a humble yet challenging motto: "Revell doesn't need me to be successful, but perhaps I have the odd idea about how to make the brand and the products even more attractive."

Andreas A. Berse

The boxer buggy!

I knew Revell when I was a lad, but things changed dramatically from 1970.

As a young hobbyist I discovered something interesting in an American magazine: the EMPI Imp dune buggy with optional Porsche 911 engine. Revell had both in its 1:25 program. So I purchased the buggy and ordered the Porsche parts from Department "X" at Bünde – for the cost of five deutschmarks in stamps.

Two days later I received a call from a certain Mr Taubert from product development. In his deep voice he said: "We've sent the five marks back to you. When you've finished the thing just send us a photo." That's how I met Ulli Taubert, without either knowing the formidable man or the Revell veteran's equally as impressive stature. As the chief editor of MODELL FAHRZEUG since 1990, I was able to publish many crazy stories about Revell, which was huge fun. One adventure took us to Hong Kong, another to hard-drinking Denmark. At some point I promised him: "If you ever want to make a book about this I'll help you."

I've now fulfilled that promise: trying to tell the story of Revell from Bünde at last, and with the help of contemporary witnesses who have been associated with and experienced the company for 50 years. And again there was one thing in particular that stands out above all else: it was fun. That's what I wish you with this book.

Andreas A. Berse

Loyal companion: Already as a kid, Andreas A. Berse assembled cars out of Revell kits. That's how he met Ulli Taubert. As the chief editor of MODELL FAHRZEUG he wrote many stories about this great brand from the East Westphalian town of Bünde.

It began in the bathtub …

… it was Easter 1956. On my first day of school I received a model kit of the U.S.S. Nautilus.

The name Revell was on the box, which didn't mean much to me at that time. My father had built model kits, which I then played with at bathtime. But I soon became so fascinated with this hobby that I bought more kits of my own. Because I lived close to Gütersloh airport, I developed a passion for Royal Air Force jets. At that time, of course, I never thought that Revell would play a significant role later in my life. After moving from Gütersloh to Bünde I joined Revell as an apprentice in preparation for taking up a course of studies. Over my 50 years at Revell I always maintained contact to the 'scene' and over the years I got to know a lot of people, all of whom were kind, easy-going and humble. During my visits, meetings, exhibitions and company trips, I always knew I'd hear historical model kit stories that were often shared on these occasions. I always vowed to collect the anecdotes and episodes from my Revell life and write a book about it, to take readers on a journey through their own modeling past. I hope this book evokes memories of a wonderful time spent with the world's most beautiful hobby. I wish you many happy hours with this book.

Ulli Taubert

Head and heart: Ulli Taubert stayed true to Revell for 50 years and during this half century had a significant impact on the brand from Bünde. Using his head and his heart, he shaped its program and products.

Bibliographic information published by the Deutsche Nationalbibliothek
The Deutsche Nationalbibliothek lists this publication in the Deutsche Nationalbibliografie; detailed bibliographic data are available in the Internet at http://dnb.dnb.de.

1st edition
ISBN 978-3-667-11393-1

Overall concept/idea/wording: Andreas A. Berse

Translation: Kaye Mueller
Editor: Hanno Vienken
Cover design and layout: Jörg Weusthoff, Weusthoff Noël, Hamburg

Photos
Bildarchiv Revell: 11, 16, 18, 19, 42-49, 52, 54, 58-129, 132-135, 141, 143, 156, 158, 161-163, 168/169, 171-173
Sarah Böke: 8, 9, 11, 18, 20, 21, 24-60, 62-70, 72-75, 79, 81, 89, 96, 117, 145-147, 155, 157
Markus Bolsinger: 128, 136-139, 148-153, 164-167, 174-175
Privatarchiv Schöneberg: 12-15, 37, 38, 40, 41, 42, 46, 47
Ulli Taubert: 130-131, 140, 144, 154, 159-160, 170
Christian Hoffmann: 17, 141
K.D. Nowack: cover, 128, 162, back cover

These photo credits were compiled with utmost care, however it cannot be ruled out that some copyright holders have not been identified. Information about possible claims should be addressed to the publisher.

Lithography: Mohn Media, Gütersloh
Printed by: print consult, Munich
Printed in Czech Republic 2018

Delius Klasing Verlag, Siekerwall 21, 33602 Bielefeld, Germany
Phone: +49-521-559-0, Fax: +49-521-559-115
Email: info@delius-klasing.de
www.delius-klasing.de

1956 1957 1958 1959

1964 1965 1966 1967

1972 1973 1974 1975

1980 1981 1982 1983

1988 1989 1990 1991

1996 1997 1998 1999

2004 2005 2006 200